CW01432573

Life,
Death &
Getting
Dressed

Life, Death & Getting Dressed

How to love your clothes... and yourself

Rebecca Willis

NR

Published in 2024 by New River Books
www.newriverbooks.co.uk

10 9 8 7 6 5 4 3 2 1

A CIP catalogue record for this book is available from the British Library.

ISBN: 978-1-915780-10-2

Cover design: Holly Ovenden
Illustrations: Rebecca Willis

Printed and bound in the UK by CPI.

This FSC label means that materials used for the product have been responsibly sourced.

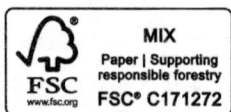

FSC®
MIX
Paper | Supporting
responsible forestry
FSC
www.fsc.org
FSC® C171272

In memory of my father, Michael,
who improbably produced a clothes-loving daughter,
and for Nick, Joe and Sam,
whatever they're wearing

CONTENTS

Guilt–edged

I used to feel bad about loving clothes. Somewhere inside, not quite in my conscious mind but not quite subconsciously either, I judged myself for it. I put myself in the dock and found myself guilty as charged, and the charges were these: being trivial and shallow, wasting time that could be better spent, having a "women's-magazine mind", being vain, materialistic and self-indulgent and – a big one, this – being different from men, with whom we were at last supposed to be equal.

In short, clothes were a guilty pleasure.

This court hearing took place in private, inside my head. I didn't discuss it with anyone or dissect it with my friends; it didn't occur to me to make it the subject of conversation or enquiry. To a teenager it seemed to be what you were meant to feel: it was just there, in the air you breathed. It was not until many years later that I began to realise where all that judgement was coming from: centuries of cultural conditioning, of society judging women on how they look, and then judging them again for caring about how they look – a twofold curse. While I was growing up, compressed aeons of complex clothing-related messages had seeped into my head.

The result? A Gordian knot of conflicting feelings and emotions, double messages and self-censorship – a pull-push, I-want-to-but-I-shouldn't, naughty-but-nice tangle that can take the rest of a lifetime to unpick. That's if you can manage to tease the threads apart enough to see them separately.

This book is a record of the threads I've managed to isolate and put under the microscope, along with other reflections on our crazy, dysfunctional, love-hate relationship with our clothes. It tackles the enduring mysteries of the wardrobe: why do we open it up in the morning and see countless garments that feel… well, slightly wrong? It explores why fashion exists, how it works and what it does to us.

I want to understand why we care so much about what we put on our bodies, why we make so many bad buys and why we often stand in front of the mirror frenziedly trying on one outfit after another before we feel ready to go out and face the world. I want to analyse why clothes have the power to make us feel so elated and so disappointed, so hopeful and so despairing, so invincible and so vulnerable.

I want to find out why we have so many clothes and nothing to wear.

The empty wardrobe

Let's stand in front of your wardrobe together. I will guess what you see.

- A pair of shoes you lusted after but you can't really walk or even stand in.

- A wool jumper that was meant to be a wardrobe staple but is "dry-clean only".

- An interesting top that you don't often wear because it requires a specialised bra that makes you feel trussed up like a chicken.

- Straight/skinny/wide/flared jeans that were once bang on trend.

- A sexy black dress that was obviously designed for someone who doesn't need to breathe.

- A pair of box-fresh trainers that made you open a fresh box of plasters before you gave up trying to break them in.

- Something so cheap you worry it was made in a sweatshop.

- An animal-print jacket that was thrilling when you bought it and now looks tawdry.

- An exquisite, long evening dress that you've never actually worn but might need one day so can't throw out.

- Sensible, office-y trousers that should be so useful but make you feel frumpy.

- Lots of trousers (or it might be tops) that accentuate the parts of your body you don't like – the parts of you that surely no one could possibly like…

There will also be a handful of trusty garments that are the workhorses of your wardrobe – the success stories that function as your sartorial security blankets. But these will be in a considerable minority. It is just one of the many puzzling things about clothes that when you first encounter them, as when you meet a new person, you have no idea what role they will play in your life. They might turn out to be a passing acquaintance or they might become a lifelong friend. You might never speak to them again. You just can't tell, and it seems to bear no relation to the amount of money you spend or how long and hard you reflect beforehand. Which is why I use my son's old suit jacket, rescued from the Oxfam pile, more often than the ridiculously similar one I agonised over before splurging on.

I smiled when I first saw a T-shirt saying: "I've been shopping all my life and haven't got a thing to wear."

Then I felt sad. Same with the ones that say "Born to shop." Why is it accepted as a matter of simple fact that our destiny, as women, is to feel that we need more stuff, particularly in our wardrobes?

I make a habit of asking women if they ever feel they have nothing to wear, and – young or old, rich or poor, fashionable or not – if they live in the so-called developed world it's nearly always the same story: despite wardrobes brimming with clothes, nothing "works", nothing magically makes them feel OK about themselves (although something new might fix it...). Even the women who profess not to care about clothes will usually admit that they're planning to buy something new for, say, their nephew's wedding and that it will make them feel more special than something rootled out of the back of the cupboard.

I call this nothing-to-wear feeling "wardrobe dysmorphia" because – as with body dysmorphia, which is surely a close cousin – it is a distortion in the mind that makes us perceive things as they are not. Thin looks fat and full looks empty. Wardrobe dysmorphia has almost nothing to do with what is in the wardrobe and almost everything to do with what is in the head of its beholder. Getting dressed is a moment of transition, when we choose how to present ourselves to the world, and it becomes a lightning rod for anxiety, discontent and self-doubt. The cultural messages we pick up about clothes are as complex and layered as the ones we pick up about our bodies, the crucial difference being that we can change our clothes far more easily than we can change our bodies. And so we do.

To strip wardrobe dysmorphia back to its bare bones and understand it, we'll need to dip our toes into subjects such as evolution, psychology and neuroscience, as well as body shape, body image, the history of clothes, social attitudes and the pressures of modern life... not forgetting the plight of the planet and the power of the patriarchy.

When we've done that, I'm hoping that you might look into your wardrobe and see it as it is, without the distortion: full of wearable clothes that speak of you but not for you, that enhance you but do not define you.

Fashion victims

My first proper job was at *Vogue*, and it gave me a front-row seat to watch fashion's front row when it wasn't sitting in the actual front row at the collections. When I left after a decade and a half, at the turn of the millennium, I had worked for four different editors-in-chief. In case you're going to ask me what working for Anna Wintour was like (most people do), some of what you'll have heard is true. She wore dark glasses indoors even on the greyest of London days, had an amazing eye (metaphorically speaking – you couldn't see her actual eyes, obviously), and meetings with her could be unnerving: on one occasion, feedback on an article I'd written consisted of her pointing at it and saying: "I got bored around here." On the other hand, she promoted me when she and the person who preceded me as travel editor had an allergic reaction to each other, she forgave me when I made mistakes, she let me take as much time off as I needed when my brother was in hospital and she commissioned me to write for her when she returned to New York (or rather she got one of her people to commission me).

The editor before her had been Beatrix Miller, who'd taken the helm in 1964. She had the aura of an especially formidable headmistress. Swathed in Jean Muir and smoke from the cigarette permanently clamped in her red-nailed fingers, she was addressed by lowly worms like me as "Miss Miller". The next editor, Liz Tilberis, was like Anna Wintour, she had a brilliant visual sense, but she was pretty much the opposite in personality – always smiley, encouraging and friendly – and rarely edited a single word. Her successor, Alexandra Shulman, who went on to become British *Vogue*'s longest-serving editor, was clever, frank and funny, a real writer's editor with acute journalistic instincts. In their vastly differing and sometimes scary ways, they were all good editors to work for and to learn from.

And then there were the clothes. In the blond-wood corridors of Vogue House, fashion editors and their young assistants scurried around with rails of garments, treating them with high seriousness and an infectious excitement. But although they might enthuse about the frocks and the fabulousness, I couldn't help noticing that most didn't themselves try to keep up with every trend that they turned into a "story" for the fashion pages. Indeed, many seemed to have settled on a particular look and developed a sort of personal uniform. Grace Coddington, a hugely influential creative force at *Vogue* for many decades, wore her signature black trousers and shirt every day. It appeared that toiling up close to the whirling merry-go-round of fashion meant you didn't actually have to climb aboard; it was as if they acknowl-edged the impossibility of trying to keep up, or perhaps even felt above it all. The magazine's readers might have been surprised to know that the people involved in disseminating fashion's twists and turns were not slavishly following it. All this made me think about the industry and how it works.

Wanting to wear something new was probably harmless enough once upon a time – in Jane Austen's day, say, when shopping meant a trip to the local town to choose ribbon for your bonnet. The haberdasher had to make a living and the purchase was a straightforward transaction that would have felt, more or less, like a fair exchange. He or she was not aiming for global market domination in their particular brand of ribbon. In the modern world, with its galloping consumerism and microchip technology, shopping has become an unfair fight. Even at a glance, the battle lines look decidedly unequal.

On one side: billion-dollar, multinational empires with voracious financial appetites, vast advertising and marketing budgets and the ability to flash trends around the world in a split second, churn out acres of cheap new clothes in a few weeks and sell them to us in our bedrooms when we should be asleep. These huge corporations strategically place products in films and pay celebrities and social media influencers, so that we're being marketed at even when we think we're relaxing. And when we are online they employ "programmatic advertising", which in a nanosecond uses an algorithm to target us with "relevant" ads. Sure, we've inadvertently conspired in this, because – curious, social animals that we are – we've handed over masses of data about ourselves in exchange for "free" use of the internet. We didn't realise it was like falling in with the retail version of the Taliban. And, as a consequence, we are targeted more precisely, more mercilessly and more manipulatively than at any other time in history. The fashion industry, in short, has some very big guns.

Lined up on the other side, with our penknives and plastic swords, are you and I, small and defenceless against such a colossal assault. What chance do we stand? Our ribbon-buying years are not so long ago and our minds are not properly equipped for this battle – not least because, due to the very nature of fashion – its need to keep moving on – that fight is never finished. It's an exhausting war of attrition, enacted in ways so thoroughly integrated into modern life that it is hard to escape even if we manage to gain the necessary objectivity to want to. And meanwhile, it is hurting our brains, our bank balances and our planet.

As with any battle, reportage from the front lines can be unreliable and partisan. You could be forgiven for assuming that the fashion press is on our side and exists to offer consumers independent advice and analysis, in the same way that news organisations (ideally) relay the news. But it turns out fashion journalism is sleeping with the enemy.

The fashion media – in print and online – are cogs in the very machine they report on: they will never tell you with much conviction that you don't need to shop. They might fleetingly espouse vintage clothing or run a feature by someone who didn't buy anything new for a whole year. But mostly they are appealing to our unconscious appetites by whipping up excitement about new things, creating an attractive environment for advertisers whose products we might then buy – sorry, "invest in". The fashion media survives by generating consumer cravings for advertisers to satisfy.

In newspapers, where the news pages are full of all manner of apocalyptic, climate-related disasters affecting the planet – droughts, wildfires and floods – the features pages will, without apparent irony, encourage us to shop, with articles on "best buys now" and "autumn's must-haves" and "this season's colour". Note how time is always mentioned ("now"/"this season"/"autumn") to convey a sense of fashion's forward movement that confines your existing clothes firmly to the past. And they use themselves as evidence: "Have we reached peak white trainers? The fashion pack have already ditched them." We swallow this disconnect, partly because – as we'll see later – our brains really want to.

Here's an illustration from personal experience of how things have changed over recent decades. When I first worked at *Vogue*, the magazine confidently dominated its sector of the market, and maintained the illusion of a strict division between the editorial and advertising parts of the publication. The editorial side was proudly creative and independent and regarded the advertising side as a sort of grubby trade that paid the bills but was rather an embarrassment, like a rich but vulgar relation. Paying for an advert did not guarantee that your clothes would be featured in a fashion shoot.

There was, however, a promotions department that blurred this supposedly fixed line, with paid-for pages designed to look like editorial; the untrained eye could easily miss the small print at the top of the page pointing out this subtle distinction. And over time, as more and more fashion magazines were launched, the pressure from advertisers became increasingly overt. When one big brand complained that its clothes were never featured on shoots, the fashion editor eventually agreed to use one of its coats but first lopped a huge chunk off the bottom with a pair of scissors – thereby triggering another storm of complaint.

By the time I left the magazine in 1999, there was a person whose full-time job was to liaise between advertising and editorial to ensure that the advertisers were kept happy and didn't jump ship to some upstart rival publication. The truth is that the fashion media has always been at the behest of fashion's big players, whatever it may have feigned, in order to borrow the clothes, to get the previews and the stories and the seats in the front row. And today, there is no longer any pretence that commerce isn't driving the fashion coverage: what started as an awkward embrace with an avoidant air-kiss has become a symbiotic merger and ultimately a take-over. It's a microcosm of the way commerce has infiltrated our lives, exerting influence at every turn.

So, one giant reason we feel we have nothing to wear is that the fashion industry keeps telling us so – playing on our insecurities with all its ingenuity and through every channel it possibly can. But simply persuading us to buy more clothes across the board is not enough. Each of the constituent parts of the fashion industry, each separate brand, needs us to buy more of its own clothes as opposed to its rivals'. There's an internecine arms race going on, and it's this commercial competition between different brands that really ramps up the pressure on us, as they jostle for our attention and our money, striving to annex the territory of our minds. The really big companies hedge their bets and launch several shops aimed at slightly different sectors of the market to make sure they can't lose – the H&M group owns Cos, Arket and & Other Stories (& other brands), while Inditex, which owns Zara, also has Pull & Bear, Massimo Dutti, Bershka and Stradivarius. The brutal truth is that, although it permeates our lives and affects our sense of self, we as individuals are not personally involved in this ruthless corporate fight for survival. We're not even cannon fodder, just innocent bystanders caught in the crossfire.

Next time you find yourself gazing hopelessly into your wardrobe, remember it's not surprising you feel panicked. You are being fought over, like a piece of meat in the middle of a pack of wild dogs, by powerful forces that are in turn fighting for their own commercial existence.

The thin of it

Fashion does not, unfortunately, stop with what we wear. It spills over onto our very flesh and bones. Physical appearance has always mattered to some extent. For millions of years, as with all animals, it has been an indicator of health and important for mate selection. (It's been suggested, though, that facial beauty was not important until sex evolved into a face-to-face encounter, missionary position, rather than doggy-style.) As human society has gradually become more intricate, the body has become increasingly idealised and itself subject to fashion.

The ideal figure is very much a product of its time, as the following two examples show. Queen Victoria, barely five feet tall, was the uber-influencer of her day and started a vogue for smallness and daintiness: women wore flat slippers to be as short as possible. Paintings made two hundred years earlier by the great Baroque artist, Peter Paul Rubens, show that an ample covering of flesh was highly desirable in the 17th century, a time when most people couldn't afford to be so well-fed.

So how did we get from short and fat to where we are today? To answer that, we need to take a brisk trot through the 20th century because, in the 1920s, the bust-to-waist ratio of the ideal female figure changed dramatically. It moved, probably as never before, towards boyishness: curves went out and a straight up-and-down figure came in. Fashionable women bound their breasts to appear flat-chested. This new, slender ideal reflected the huge change in the role of women after two firsts: the first wave of feminism and the First World War. They were leading more independent, active lives, and the class system was breaking down too: it's not a coincidence that suntans became fashionable at this point, now signifying a life of leisure, freedom and travel rather than a life spent labouring in the fields.

By the 1950s, after the privations of the Second World War, the pendulum had swung the other way and the well-fed, hourglass figure of Marilyn Monroe became the ideal. Adverts encouraged skinny women to take weight-gain supplements, and the bust-to-waist ratio swung back for a while. But it dropped again in the 1960s and '70s when the athletic, slim ideal really got its gracile feet under the table, upon which there was, by then, considerably more to eat. Diet and exercise slowly replaced foundation garments and girdles as a means of making the body conform to the times.

The long, beanpole decades that came next saw different types of thinness follow each other down the catwalk: there are fashions even in emaciation. After the

Amazonian supermodels of the 1980s, peak thinness was reached in the '90s with the heroin-chic of grunge and the unhealthy Hollywood obsession with "size 0"; this era cast a long shadow, helping to disorder the eating of the underweight models themselves as well as the public, who were drip-fed an unbalanced diet of their images. The 21st-century manifestation of the thinness ideal looks a little more wholesome – sleek and streamlined, with a bit more flesh and a lot more time at the gym – but it is still a tyranny that requires work and time that women might want to spend on other things, for example their actual work or their education.

When Liz Tilberis, one of the four editors-in-chief I worked for at British *Vogue*, finally lost the weight she'd been wanting to lose for years, it was because she was dying of ovarian cancer. Even knowing that she was seriously ill, she was able to write in her book that she loved "the fact that she didn't have an extraneous bump anywhere". That slimness is so often caused by stress, anxiety, bereavement and other trauma does not appear to detract from its desirability.

Just as it seemed that the needle on the dial of fashion was stuck forever on thin, I spotted in a shop a pair of women's lycra shorts with "optional butt-lets for added volume", jelly-like inserts designed to make the bottom appear bigger and more rounded. It seemed impossible, comical even, after so many years of small-bottomed hiplessness, but the "slim-thick" ideal, embodied by Kim Kardashian, had landed with a (well-cushioned) bump. Had the hourglass finally returned, albeit in near-caricature form and with a new, bootylicious name? Yes, but it too requires work. And it's just as prescriptive and unattainable for some women as skinniness has long been for others.

Trends in body shape are, like all fashions, a contrapuntal commentary on society, expressing the inverse of what is standard and available. As with the ruffs and towering wigs of previous centuries – which we'll come to later – the elite aspire to precisely what the masses are unable to have. Thus thinness is desirable in a time of plenty, when an obesity crisis is brewing, whereas fleshy curves are preferred when food is scarce. This has been shown to hold true on a micro scale, too: experiments have shown that in Western society males are more likely to prefer a larger female body size when they are hungry than when they are not. In fact, it seems that the hungrier people are, the more they're attracted to big things, full stop.

It would be nice to think that we could ignore trends in body shape, but they filter into the cultural mainstream like water through sand. They are modelled to us in adverts and movies, on billboards and red carpets. They insinuate themselves into our minds and become a yardstick against which it is almost impossible not to measure ourselves.

It can seem that beauty, like genius, is a matter of being in the right place at the right time. It's easy to feel that you've missed your moment, that there was a decade that would really have played to your strengths: I think mine might have been the late '60s, although sadly I was at junior school at the time. So it's worth reminding ourselves that the ideal body shape is a social construct and that humans have brains that mistake social constructs for truth and believe in them as if they were real.

Fashions in body shape will pass like all fashions, although we are barely aware of it happening, particularly when we are young: if you could watch the changes like a film on fast-forward, the beanpole and the hourglass and the waif would be as airy and ephemeral as clouds going by on a windy day.

Why clothes matter

Vision is our supreme sense, and humans had been communicating with gestures and grunting for millennia before there was anything that resembled what you might call speech. Today we have emojis to do the same job. There are various estimates of how much human communication is non-verbal – scientific research suggests somewhere between 50% and 90%. What we choose to wear – or are compelled to wear – is an integral part of that.

In the gap between the first loincloth and today's fashion industry – which is as great as the gap between a flint axe head and the International Space Station – clothing has become a sophisticated language in its own right. It can say things about us that we wouldn't say out loud. If I were a therapist, I'd ask my patients about clothes in the very first session. You wouldn't need to be a full-on shopaholic, using consumption to numb your feelings, for your answers to reveal a good deal about how you see yourself and the world around you. Whether you hoard or recycle, save certain items for best, leave things lying on the floor, lend clothes to your friends or buy them to hide your body, my hunch is that these behaviours are a kind of shorthand for our buried anxieties and our deeper sense of identity.

The sociobiologist Desmond Morris pointed out that "it is impossible to wear clothes without transmitting social signals". Clothing can signal where we were brought up, how we vote, how extrovert we are (or aren't), who we sleep with, which god we worship and how much we earn. When we meet someone new, we interpret this information without even registering that we're doing it, so skilled have we become at reading sartorial clues. To experience the full power of clothes, perhaps try wearing a complete stranger's clothes for a day and see how disorientating it feels. We're all fluent in clothes without knowing it.

The language of clothes has a past tense, too. Mark Twain said "naked people have little or no influence in society", and an unclothed version of history is hard to imagine. It is impossible to conceive of the Romans without their togas, Henry VIII without his slashed-and-padded doublet, soldiers without their uniforms or Queen Victoria without her widow's weeds. And clothes don't just illustrate what happened in the past; they are part of the meaning and sometimes even the cause of it. They tell the story of civilisation. They speak of the rise and fall of empires, the power of kings, the sweep of conquest, the importance of geography, the forces of climate, the convention of binary gender, the oppression of minorities and of women.

Whether in Mao's China or the court of the Sun King

or on the battlefield of the Roundheads and the Cavaliers, clothing has always articulated the values and aspirations of particular cultures. And it's a two-way street: clothes have a psychological effect on us when we put them on. They can make us feel more confident for a job interview, more purposeful when we dress smartly, more special when we dress up. They can feel like armour in which to face the world or a familiar embrace to fall into when we're relaxed and off-duty.

So clothes really do matter. Without clothes we couldn't read people as we do; we would have difficulty classifying them. And I use that word advisedly, because how we dress has for most of history been a primary indicator of class and economic status. Status and clothing are inseparable from each other. Even today, when clothing seems democratised, you only have to scratch the surface to see that status is still involved in the meaning of what we wear. Hold on to that thought, because it'll come up again. And again.

The lost charm bracelet

If you are given a piece of jewellery in the morning and you lose it that same afternoon, you feel less upset – I think I can safely say – than if you lose it after you've worn it every day for 50 years. Time and memory affect how we feel about our belongings. And other people's: why else do my eyes prick when I read in the papers that someone I've never met has been reunited with their long-lost engagement ring?

When I was a baby, I was given a charm bracelet, an item popularised by Queen Victoria but with its very long roots in prehistoric amulet-wearing. This bracelet was empty but over the years I was given various charms to put on it: a tiny tennis racquet, a dog that looked a bit (but not very) like ours, a court shoe with a heel when I was old enough to wear them, a miniature key for my 21st birthday. Later, when I earned my own money, I sometimes bought a charm and added it to the bracelet: a totem pole reminded me of a best friend in Canada, a gondola of my first, awestruck visit to Venice. So when it was stolen in a burglary, I felt I'd lost not just the physical object but also the story of my life.

Clothes too narrate our lives. They are more than a

mere diary made of fabrics and styles that remind us of what we wore when. They are part of our identity and our sense of self – that's why it's so hard to throw them out. And why it's impossible even for the most ardent nature-lover to forgive the moths that ate through a favourite jumper. And why people hang onto their wedding dresses with the persistence, if not the mood, of Miss Havisham. And why a widow, who lost her firefighter husband on 9/11, says she packed away all the clothes she wore with her husband because "that was my life with him", and it was over.

To see clearly the emotional significance of your clothes you can play a kind of sartorial Desert Island Discs and try to capture your life in eight garments. You can make a charm bracelet out of them. My selection includes the following: a poncho with an Aztec vibe knitted by my adored godmother; a white, wet-look skirt with braces that I still can't believe my mother bought me; a red school hat so identifiable that people would phone the headmistress to report us for eating in the street; a pair of navy corduroy Levi's that left me bereft whenever they were in the wash; long, black Prada boots made of neoprene that could make any outfit sassy; a sparkly, gold, second-hand dress I wore to get married in; and two pairs of black trousers to represent the endless pairs of black trousers – in every possible style from exercise leggings to palazzo pants – that have long been the beating heart of my adult wardrobe (that's almost certainly cheating, I know, but I just couldn't pick one pair).

I've had to ignore several other contenders, some of which were made by my own hand: the white satin suit I sewed when I was 17 that even Debbie Harry couldn't have carried off; the flared jeans I converted to drainpipes tight as sausage skins. Also, because memory is impressionistic and selective rather than an objective record, these clothes are only a version of my life. Like any biography, I could pick out different elements to tell a slightly different story. I could choose garments that show me in a different light, I could attach different charms to the bracelet. I could offer you a drier version – dates and places, exam results and career moves. But as source material to capture the essence of a life story? Our clothes are hard to beat.

Getting dressed for the first time

It was hard for archaeologists to know precisely when we started to wear clothes, because clothing is perishable – fabric and furs rot away long before they can turn into fossils; even synthetic fabrics will eventually biodegrade, although it may take a few hundred years.

Until, that is, lice came to the rescue.

Clothes lice are different from head lice; they evolved from them, so calculating when the two types diverged gives a good idea of when clothing appeared on the scene. There's still no absolute agreement on the matter, and anyway learning to dress ourselves would have been a slow and gradual process, with clothing at first so rudimentary that it barely deserved the name, but somewhere around 170,000 years ago seems to be the consensus. That's a few hundred thousand years after the emergence of modern humans and a few hundred thousand years before the last Ice Age. In other words, we've been getting dressed, in some form or another, for a very long time.

Why we needed clothes in the first place has also been the subject of much academic head-scratching. Not long ago – at least compared to the age of the planet

– our species was covered in hair like the great apes. We had to lose most of this hair before we needed clothes, and there are various theories that try to explain why we did so.

The heat theory suggests that, when our human ancestors moved from cool, shady forests to the open savannah, body hair made them too hot, especially for hunting in the daytime, and so it began to disappear. The fact that we became very good at sweating, with many more sweat glands than other primates, supports this idea. Then there's a theory that the parasites that lived in our body hair carried harmful and potentially deadly viruses, to the point where it was safer to have no hair. Another suggestion is that loss of hair, particularly facial hair, enabled us to read emotions in skin colouring (blushes, flushes of rage) and therefore to communicate better. And then there's the invention of fire, which gave us a direct source of heat to survive cold nights without hair, and – because we learned to cook – also the extra calories to keep our glabrous bodies warm.

Whatever the reason, and it could be a combination of these, we lost our furry covering in most places. We kept it on our heads, it's presumed for protection from the sun, and around our genitals, probably in order to reduce friction during sex, for genital temperature regulation and maybe even to retain mate-attracting pheromones. It isn't known when this permanent moult happened, but it's possible that the study of pubic lice will one day reveal how long ago they got stranded on their own little genital Galapagos island down there.

Just as hairlessness must have given early humans an evolutionary advantage, so the wearing of clothes must also have improved our fitness – in the Darwinian survival-of-the fittest sense, where fitness means most fitted to survive in its environment, not most often at Pilates. Once we'd become naked apes, clothes offered a sun screen and protection from other "weather events" as they're now called, and also from sharp objects – a puncture wound that went septic could be fatal, whether delivered by the tusk of a mammoth or a tiny thorn. Clothes also provided insulation, as fur once had, but unlike fur we could put them on and take them off and wear more or less of them, which made us adaptable to different climates.

If we hadn't worked out how to get dressed, our species might not have got very far from the dust bowl of Africa. So don't let anyone tell you clothes don't matter.

Survival mode

Forget the Oscars and the Met Gala. Probably the greatest example of sartorial showing-off took place on 7th June 1520 near Calais, when Henry VIII met Francis I of France for the first time. There followed 18 days of festivities and tournaments, during which competitive power-dressing played a crucial role: the camp was awash with rich fabrics and jewels. One day, Francis wore expensive tissue cloth encrusted with pearls; Henry soon trumped it with an outfit dripping with gold embellishments. His retinue officially numbered almost 4,000 people and Catherine of Aragon's a further 1,000 – not to mention the thousands of workers who built the tents and the king's temporary palace, and almost 3,000 horses – so it's little wonder that the whole occasion is estimated to have cost the English crown a seventh of its annual income. The tent hangings, furnishings and opulent garments made such extravagant use of the costliest of cloths – a mixture of silk and a thread spun with real gold – that the entire summit became known as the Field of the Cloth of Gold.

I bring this up because it helps illustrate the answer to the question that follows the one about why we wear clothes at all, namely, why do clothes have a function beyond the functional? Or, in other words, what is the evolutionary point of fashion? To have survived for so long – long enough, anyway, to grow into the bloated behemoth of today's industry – it must, at least once upon a time, have conferred an evolutionary advantage.

Darwin's second great insight after natural selection was his theory of sexual selection – the ability of an individual to attract a mate and ensure genetic survival (because what's the point in developing opposable thumbs if you don't have kids to pass them on to?). The competition between males for females explained traits that were not about mere survival: the lion's mane, the stag's branching antlers and the plumage of the male bird of paradise. Broadly speaking, in the rest of the animal kingdom, members of one sex successfully mate when they show themselves to be stronger or sexier than their peers. In humans, both sexes take part in reproductive competition, and clothing plays its part in this. It's often said that "women dress for each other", but in purely evolutionary terms "because of each other" would be more accurate. It's because of sexual competition, which by the way also explains the phenomenon of the "friend" who doesn't want to tell you where she bought her dress.

A quick aside, while we're on the subject of evolution. People often wonder why the "plumage" of human males is more muted than that of females, whereas in wild animals it seems the other way about. This observation is based on the very specific culture of the industrialised world and is not borne out by the history of dress or in other cultures. In the West, extreme male display has been largely displaced onto externals such as fast cars and big houses – think of a red Ferrari as the robin's red breast. It also ignores the fact that display includes behavioural as well as visual traits: risk-taking in males has been shown to increase in the company of females and signals high testosterone – it's the fast car again, or Henry and Francis jousting. And anyway, rappers are doing a good job of blinging up menswear following the dunnocky boring-suit era instigated by Beau Brummell a few centuries ago. But that's another story.

Because display is a survival tool, in genetic terms, it means that survival and how we look are profoundly linked, and it's one big reason fashion is hard to resist. Humans are visually oriented primates who have learned how to use clothing to gain competitive advantage. And maintaining this advantage when others start to imitate it is one of the factors that keeps fashion moving on and changing.

The competition for survival determines the structure of society: humans tend to live in hierarchies, whether the structure of it is steep – with a royal family at one end and homeless people sleeping on the streets at the other, to pick a random example – or whether it is relatively shallow and striving for equality. For social animals like us, living in a group means we are more likely to survive, successfully raise our young (who are born relatively helpless compared to other mammals) and pass on our genes. The advantages of group living are multiplied for individuals who have high status within that group: they are especially protected by the others and, in societies that allow harem behaviour (i.e. multiple reproductive partners), they have greater opportunity to pass on their genes.

Because moving on up is beneficial, aspiration is an inherent part of a hierarchical social system – even today, in the developed world, social status has a documented effect on health and longevity. Communism and kibbutzes in their purest forms have failed because people aspired to more. Scientists have tried to determine whether the desire for status is a fundamental motive in humans, or whether it's merely a by-product of the need to belong. And, having reviewed hundreds of studies involving people of different cultures, genders, ages and personalities, they concluded that status is something that everyone craves and covets, "even if they don't realise it". In other words, we're hard-wired to aspire.

There's an Italian proverb that says that after the game the king and the pawn go back in the same box. But in life as in chess, social position affects how you proceed across the board until that moment. Studies have shown that humans don't just want higher status; they want higher status *than other people*. It's relative to others, hence the phenomenon of keeping up with the Joneses – and what they are wearing. A quick way to signal the progress we're making is by owning things. Whether it's more goats and camels, a Picasso and a private jet, a designer handbag and a new dress, the underlying drive is the same. Status and clothing are woven indivisibly together: the fabric of society.

Clothing has a great advantage over other forms of display: it is portable. You can't carry about your person a large house, acres of land or a luxury hotel, nor can you take a sports car indoors. Clothing is used as symbolic communication, and we can interpret it because as humans we have the unique cognitive ability to sense intention: we can attach meaning to self-adornment in a way that other animals cannot.

The most obvious way to get the message across is to use rare and expensive materials, as we saw with Henry's outfit dripping with gold – I know, Tudors again, but they make the point so clearly (as Antonia Fraser writes in *The Six Wives of Henry VIII*, "in the Tudor court, dress was the medium to convey the message"). Today's equivalent might be a gold Rolex or a pair of diamond-studded trainers – although some of their value comes from marketing rather than the scarcity of the materials used. Marketing works because humans are highly suggestible: it's been shown, for instance, that wine tastes better when we believe it to be expensive.

My favourite story illustrating display-through-scarcity-value concerns a string of pearls. Before cultured pearls were invented, they had to be found in the wild and were therefore rare and valuable: it took many years for a jeweller to collect and match them, and as a visual manifestation of wealth they were second to none. So it was that in New York in 1917, the jeweller Pierre Cartier did a deal with the railroad magnate Morton F Plant. Cartier gave Plant a double-string necklace of South Sea pearls that Plant's wife Maisie had her eye on, and in exchange Plant gave Cartier his enormous mansion at 653 Fifth Avenue. The building, a whopping slice of Manhattan real estate, has been Cartier's US flagship ever since. The pearls, when auctioned almost 40 years later after cultured pearls had become widely available, fetched just US$151,000. It remains to be seen whether the invention of synthetic diamonds will devalue the natural rocks in a similar way. Possibly not, since their scarcity is artificial, with supply controlled by big corporations such as De Beers. Limited editions of clothes or handbags work in the same way, with deliberate scarcity contriving to increase demand and create waiting lists.

Another way to convey high status is by wearing clothes that are labour-intensive to make: royal wedding dresses are the prime example of this. The lace is "hand-made" and the number of ornaments and the number of hours it took to attach them are drooled over by the commentators. Queen Elizabeth II wore a Norman Hartnell dress that took 350 women seven weeks to make and was adorned with 10,000 seed pearls. That's hard to beat as a status symbol, although designer couture has a go: it's estimated that today only a few thousand women in the world can afford couture dresses, so buying one is like paying for membership of a club to which only about 0.0001% of the world's population can belong.

None of this is new. In the Upper Paleolithic burial site at Sunghir, discovered in 1955 to the east of Moscow, many thousands of mammoth ivory beads were unearthed with the human skeletons. It's not known what the beads signified but what seems certain is that, for those hunter-gatherers 30,000 years ago, they conferred some kind of distinction. Furthermore, it is estimated that they took an estimated 7,500 hours to make, which I think qualifies them as labour-intensive.

When Lady Diana Spencer married Prince Charles, her shoes alone were decorated with 542 sequins and 132 pearls. The fact that they were mostly obscured by the meringue-like skirts of her bouffant dress did not matter. It was the fact of them rather than the sight of them that was important. The visual "waste" of the shoes actually added to their significance, which brings us to the intriguing subject of clothes and the deliberate squandering of resources.

Clothes for not working in

When people look at catwalk photos and exclaim: "That's so impractical! No one would ever wear that!", they are entirely missing the point. Impracticality is part of these clothes' raison d'être, because clothing can proclaim that you don't need to do physical work yourself and thus signal your superiority.

There are parallels in the animal kingdom, the peacock's tail being a good example. It illustrates an evolutionary theory from 1975 known as the handicap principle, which suggests that with its tail the peacock is saying: "Look at me, I've got this unnecessary, extravagant appendage because I've gone way beyond merely surviving. I'm rich as Croesus, a man of leisure. You won't find a better reproductive partner than me." It is showing that the bird can squander its resources, just as humans do by conspicuous consumption.

Humans have come up with some truly fantastic and absurd pieces of clothing over the centuries to do the job of encumbering and impeding the wearer (the word "impede" comes from the Latin root meaning "to shackle the feet"). While we take a look at some of them, it's worth remembering that the history of fashion, like all history, was written by the victors – the social victors, that is. When we imagine the clothing of Ancient Rome or Georgian England, chances are we are picturing what the privileged elite was wearing. They were the people who could afford to follow fashion and to patronise artists to record them wearing it. The painted portrait was a kind of meta-display – a display of a display – and itself a status symbol; when John Singer Sargent hiked up his fees because he had too many commissions, he found himself more in demand than ever.

The skeletons of medieval Britons tell us that a surprising number of them suffered from bunions, because they insisted on wearing long, pointy shoes called *poulaines*. So called because they originated in Poland, those worn by men could measure up to 60cm and were stuffed with moss and whalebone to keep them stiff. Ignoring the phallic symbolism here, walking in these shoes must have been like wearing flippers on dry land, which is no mean feat. In the same era, people wore sleeves so long and wide that sometimes they had to be knotted to stop them dragging on the ground. Sleeve length was literally a measure of how much material you could afford.

Poulaines were primarily a male form of display, but more often than not (because a status symbol for men was – and sometimes still is – having an idle and decorative wife), the weight of this sort of display fell onto women. And it still does today, even though women now make up more than half the workforce.

During the Renaissance, women wore platform shoes called *chopines* that could be up to half a metre high: the increased height meant longer dresses and thus more fabric could be used to display the family wealth, turning wives and daughters into human billboards. The women wearing these vertiginous shoes needed a servant or two to support them – an arrangement that was a veritable diagram of social hierarchy. One of the many remarkable things at the funeral of Queen Elizabeth II was the alpine height of the royal wives' footwear. It's a fair bet that no one in the ten-mile queue to view her coffin was similarly shod.

If you had to think of the least practical thing to keep near your face, particularly while you're eating, you might well come up with something like the ruff: a stiff, white, intricately folded collar that framed the head and could in extreme cases project so far out from the neck that it took up more square footage than the body to which it was attached. In their 16th-century heyday, wearers of these piccadills (from which Piccadilly in London gets its name) sometimes had to use extra-long spoons, or eat before they went out. Keeping them clean, starched and ironed was time-consuming, although of course it wasn't the time of the wearer that was consumed. And, like most fashions designed to demonstrate that there's absolutely no chance of manual work being undertaken, ruffs also affected the physical bearing of the wearers: they forced people to hold themselves stiffly and apart, to be literally standoffish.

Tall wigs, and indeed any accessory that exaggerates height, deliberately create the impression of aloofness. Balancing something on your head, or yourself on high heels, demands a self-conscious care of movement that is in itself a luxury. As with the ruff, when it came to the 150-year craze for wigs that began in the 17th century, size mattered. Wigs were expensive, so much so that people bequeathed them in their wills. The larger the wig you could afford, the higher your social standing – hence the expression "bigwig". When Samuel Pepys first went to church in a wig, he felt apprehensive and thought people would laugh. But they didn't (at least, not in front of him). One of the curious things about fashion is that innovations initially feel strange to the point of absurdity – even to the wearer, as Pepys discovered – and they seem ridiculous and comical afterwards, as the *poulaines*, wigs and ruffs do to us now, but when they are in full swing and widely adopted they seem normal and we wear them with a straight face.

Women's wigs could be two-and-a-half feet tall and might be adorned with feathers, a model of a sailing ship or an entire stuffed bird. They were itchy, uncomfortable and hot, but as encumbrances they were highly effective: women sometimes had to sit on the floor of their carriages or ride with their heads out of window. Also like the ruff, wigs were high-maintenance – they needed brushing, re-curling and powdering. In 1660 there were 200 *perruquiers* at the court of Louis XIV: wigs showed that you had other people working for you.

You needed staff, too, to lace you into a boned corset and insert you into one of the gigantic skirts that, at various times in history, have made women literally unapproachable, cordoning them off like cattle in a pen. In Victorian times, just as women's lives were circumscribed by stifling rules, so their bodies were encased in enormous skirts. The crinoline appeared in the 1850s and, cumbersome as it was, was welcomed because it weighed less than the many layers of petticoats which came before it (these could tip the scales at 18kg). As well as being an effective form of social distancing, the crinoline exaggerated the hip size which symbolised female fertility – families were large at the time. They were also the opposite of the male silhouette. Corsets, tightly laced in pursuit of the "wasp waist", intensified this contrast between the shape of men and women.

The farthingale, ancestor of the crinoline and popular from the late-sixteenth to the mid-seventeenth century, did the same job. Effectively a platform at hip level from which the skirts hung, they could be well over a metre wide – call to mind (or search online) the Infanta Margarita Theresa in Velázquez's painting *Las Meninas* (The Ladies in Waiting). It's acutely poignant to see a little child – she was probably about five years old – imprisoned in the gilded cage of her clothing as a mark of her status, which she had yet to understand.

The element of the ridiculous in these extremes forms of encumbrance tips over into something more sinister when the impediment causes permanent damage to the wearer. Witness the tight-laced corsets that crushed the internal organs and caused breathing problems; the ancient Chinese tradition of foot-binding, a distant ancestor of our bunion-causing high heels, where women's bones were broken in pursuit of dainty feet; and death by crinoline – when the huge skirts caught fire, the metal cage acted as an efficient flue.

None of this shows a very attractive aspect of human nature, in fact it barely seems sane. And yet it's all part of the Darwinian competition to survive.

Novelty value

However expensive your clothing and however obstructive your sartorial impediments, their power to convey status is hugely magnified by the simple fact of being new. To be able to afford new things, never to be seen in the same thing twice, indicates high status that is not only current but also ongoing: for prospective mates it speaks of the future. And when novelty indicates the continuation of existence, shopping becomes a survival skill.

I've never heard anyone say they have "nothing to wear" for walking the dog: it's axiomatic that the more important the occasion is, the emptier the wardrobe seems. We "need" something new to wear for landmark celebrations like weddings and 21st-birthday parties in order to mark their momentousness: novelty and specialness have become conflated in our minds. Often the only way in which our new clothes are "better" than the ones we already own is in the fact that we've never worn them before – most of the people you meet, unless you're constantly in the public eye, won't know whether you're wearing something new or not. That's why one of the functions of high fashion is to be unmistakably, outrageously new.

The royals, again, provide a useful illustration: the expectation is that they, and particularly the women, should wear something that hasn't been seen before: it helps reinforce their status in the eyes of the public and demonstrates that they are not ordinary people with budgets to consider. For the inaugural Earthshot Prize Awards, part of their initiative to "generate a global movement to repair the planet", the (then) Duke and Duchess of Cambridge "recycled" outfits that they'd worn in public before, and asked their guests not to buy new clothes for the event. It's a brilliant example to set, and I hope party-givers everywhere will follow suit. But I suspect it may be an uphill struggle, particularly – and ironically – when royalty is present and people's competitive, status-signalling buttons are being pressed with a vengeance.

When I read that Catherine Parr, my favourite of Henry VIII's wives, had bought 47 pairs of shoes in a single year, my first reaction, before I caught myself, was "lucky her!". Like Princess Diana's wedding pumps, these shoes would have been barely visible under her dresses – certainly they wouldn't have been the first thing you'd notice about her. But that, once again, is the point. The squandering of resources lies buried beneath our purchases today just as it did in Catherine Parr's shoe collection.

So, in the language of clothes, the loudest proclamation of status-and-survival is a constantly changing wardrobe

– that is one reason we walk straight into the open jaws of the retailers with our wallets hanging out, ripe for the picking. Our attraction to novelty dovetails so precisely with the need of the fashion industry to sell us new stuff that it's hard to see the join. The two fit together like pieces of a well-made jigsaw, because the industry has machine-tooled itself to exploit our survival instincts.

Why new becomes old

Imagine you're an early human, managing to survive in the grasslands of what we now call Africa. You notice something ochre-coloured behind a bush. It could be a lion or it could just be a rock. If you assume it's a lion and scarper, you may be wrong but you'll survive. If you assume it's a rock, stay put and you're wrong… well, you only make that mistake once. False positives, or Type 1 errors as they're called in statistics, are a safer bet than false negatives or Type 2 errors. The early humans who noticed changes around them, assumed the worst and took action are the ones who lived on, and their genes – including their alertness to novelty – got passed on, too. In evolutionary terms, contentment is a potentially dangerous state. Even now, when we have so much to be content about, we can't switch that instinct off. Our brains are hard-wired to notice change and to respond to it – another reason we're easy prey for fashion.

This novelty-alert, questioning brain has made *Homo sapiens* inventive and resourceful in a way that other mammals are not. It has given us the ability to invent tools and build complex civilisations – if not the wisdom to make them last. For us as a species it has been beneficial. For us as individuals, though, there's a downside, particularly when it comes to surviving in today's consumer culture. Because our minds are drawn to the area of greatest uncertainty, anything that is constantly changing grabs our attention: social media can therefore hijack our brains. Our novelty-antennae are so sensitive that a well-aimed ad campaign can convince us that we really need the latest smartphone or the just-released trainers. We even start to question our own bodies and wonder if they need changing, too – we'll look at that issue in more detail later on.

Our eyes see the lion behind the bush, but our other senses are also alert for change, like an alarm system that is fully set. When we hear a new sound or smell a new scent, we notice it and pay attention. Then we become habituated to it. Once our brains have worked out it's not a threat, we no longer register it in the same way. That's why, after a while, we don't smell the perfume or aftershave we wear as strongly as we once did, although others might be overwhelmed by it. We might even end up buying a new one.

Our wardrobes are full of once-new things that our brain no longer registers.

The Pending Shelf

Here's a way to trick our neophilic, overconsuming brains. It's based on a tip someone once gave me about clearing out the children's toys and it works with clothing, too (we learn from our offspring in unexpected ways).

It goes like this. You remove a number of toys – enough to create the space and order you need – and you hide them. In the case of toys, if they play an annoying tune or are particularly sharp when trodden on in bare feet, that's a bonus. If, after six months, they have not been missed, you can get rid of them. Alternatively, you can give a few of them back to your children, who will greet them like old friends, and the toys will enjoy a second lease of life.

All you need is a good hiding place: I put my maybe-maybe-not clothes in a bag on a shelf too high for daily use – I call it the Pending Shelf, but it could be a box in the attic or one of those zip-up plastic bags under the bed. (OK, I admit I've got a couple of bags in the attic, too, but I'm sure they must be useful as insulation). It is amazing how quickly you forget what it contains, and it makes clearing out clothes much less agonising and absolute: the ones you aren't sure about, or can't bear to part with, live in a kind of limbo or purgatory until their fate is decided.

Very occasionally your child will ask after a particular toy which you know is already in the Cancer Research shop. I admit I've pretended to search for things that were probably already being played with by another child in another house. The same can happen with clothes – one day you wish you still had that old shirt – but with the passing of time the emotional heat has gone out of it. Alternatively, sometimes you can't remember whether you've given something away or just hidden it, and when you find it again your heart lifts as if you've found a long-lost relative.

With the clothes on the Pending Shelf, there is a trial separation before the divorce goes ahead. There is still a way back. The only modification is that, when it comes to clothes as opposed to children's toys, the six-month period really needs to be extended to a year, so that you've lived through all the possible weather conditions before the Day of Judgement dawns.

And dawn it must, because ultimately it's bad karma to keep clothes you're never going to wear again. After a season in purgatory, that old dress might be given a reprieve and will feel almost like new – without any fallout for your bank balance or the ecosystem. But if absence doesn't make the heart grow fonder – and often it does quite the opposite, so that you can't believe you ever left the house in that peculiar garment – then you just give the clothes to charity or to friends. You set them free for reincarnation.

Reward points

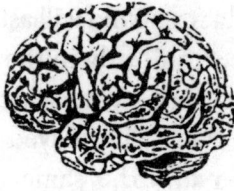

Dopamine, our brain's most famous neurotrans-mitter, is nicknamed the "feel-good hormone", but that doesn't do justice to its CV. It's involved in regulating movement, heart rate, sleep, kidney function, mood and decision making, and when it goes wrong it is associated with some serious psychiatric and neuro-logical disorders such as schizophrenia and Parkinson's disease. For our purposes, though, it's dopamine's role as a cog in our reward-motivation system that matters.

The brain's reward system is not actually designed to make you feel good, but rather to help you learn. Specifically, it "wires in" associations that influence us to behave in ways that promote our old friends, survival and reproduction. And it's got a great address book: while the average neuron is connected to 10,000 other cells, parts of the reward system have cells with 50 times that number of connections.

In simple terms, dopamine links pleasure-gener-ating things to the desire to repeat them. It activates the pathway in the mid-brain that tells you to repeat what you just did to get the reward – the reward being the euphoric feeling that accompanies, say, sex or eating chocolate or buying (another) little black dress. Dopamine encourages exploration by rewarding us when we stumble across something beneficial. It also tells the memory centre to take note, so that we can predict what will happen when we do that thing again: if I buy this dress I know I'll get a buzz.

The dopamine pathway lights up not just at the moment of purchase, but all through the anticipation that leads up to it. It's active whether we're window-shopping, browsing or clicking to buy online. With online shopping, you get a reward when you click to buy and another one when it's delivered – it's a two-for-one deal, biochemistry-wise. Some people like to experience this vicariously by watching "unboxing" videos on YouTube, which show strangers opening the packaging and taking out a new purchase – yes, it's a thing, google it. The dopamine pathway is extra busy at sale time, because the unpredictability increases anticipation and therefore dopamine release. The unexpected "40% off" sign has sucked us right in before we can read the words "Up to…" in small print that precede it.

Dopamine has a role in addiction, and although people joke about shopaholism, it really exists and is officially known as Compulsive Buying Disorder (CBD) or oniomania (from the Greek *onios,* meaning "for sale"). Research shows it gives a feeling of control when we feel powerless, and as with drugs, alcohol and gambling, sufferers can end up with huge debts and destroyed relationships. It's hard to get accurate data – not least because it's so easy to shop in secret nowadays

– but it could be that up to 20% of women in the UK are affected. Online, auction websites encourage gambling-style shopping, but in a way most shopping is gambling: unless we actually need what we're buying, we're simply betting that it will make us feel better.

The odds are that it will – for a short time. The problem with euphoria is that it wears off. That's partly because of what's called hedonic adaptation, also known as the hedonic treadmill. This refers to the way our happiness – and indeed our grief – tends after a time to return to a baseline, like a factory reset for the mood centre of the brain. It's why time heals, and also why our latest purchases fail to satisfy us for long.

Aristotle knew about this in the fourth century BCE: he distinguished between hedonic (sensory) and eudaemonic (moral) wellbeing, and recognised that the former does not last as long as the latter. He'd be pleased to know that modern science backs him up: there's now good evidence to show that pleasure derived from self-less acts tends to outlast physical pleasures. If we could teach ourselves to think only about long-term happiness, we'd give to charity instead of buying another pair of jeans. And yet the thrill of the new is so powerful that another pair of jeans seems a better idea at the time.

When we say we have nothing to wear, we mean we have nothing new to wear. It's the voice of our reward system, curled deep inside our brains, demanding a fix.

Possession

Walking into a promising-looking clothes shop is like entering Aladdin's cave – treasure all around and the possibility that a genie in a bottle will magic up the perfect thing so that the wardrobe will never seem empty again. There's nothing quite like that feeling.

Except that there is. The fluttering in the stomach, the dry mouth and the faster heartbeat: these are the same physiological symptoms caused by the same arousal hormones that flood your body when you're newly in love or gambling. Clothes shopping has a lot in common with those two activities, being also about excitement, hope and risk-taking. Just like the romantic myth of the perfect partner, it holds the twin promises of completing you and transforming your life. And, as with new love, infatuation blinds you to the thought that it might not work out. This purchase is forever...

What is this power of possessing that makes us behave as if we are ourselves possessed? We've looked at why we like having things that are new, but let's consider why we like having things at all.

In common with all animals, we need the basics – food and shelter – to survive. When humans were hunter-gatherers, we couldn't control food supply and had few belongings because we moved from place to place, finding nourishment wherever nature allowed. Our shopping skills may be in part a long hangover from our hunting and gathering days, when we chased down and collected what we needed to survive.

About 12,000 years ago, when we started to settle in one place and become agriculturalists, we began to accumulate more possessions in the form of farming-related tools and equipment. Land became a possession, too. Cultivating crops was a risky business because, if they failed, it could mean starvation. In case of drought or a failed harvest, we needed to have more than enough food put away. So we learned to prepare for the future and for the worst-case scenario. Agriculture turned us into planners and property owners, and as a by-product made us anxious and territorial and possessive.

Because human beings are inventive and ingenious, we worked out how to preserve and pickle food, to dry it and salt it. And eventually we ended up with colossal supermarkets instead of fields, and freezers in our homes. It's the same story with shelter, which most obviously consists of a roof over our heads but which also includes clothing. As we've seen, we couldn't live in certain climates without clothes, and in the same way that we stored food we must have known – particularly in colder climates – that having more clothes was a good precaution. We are drawn to clothes for survival reasons, just as our bodies are drawn to the calorie-promise of sweet food. The full larder and the full wardrobe are siblings.

Knowing that we've done what we can to increase our survival chances makes us feel safe and secure: possessions soothe our existential angst. And because survival is the opposite of death, owning things feels like a defiance of our mortal nature, even though we know we can't take them with us when we die (some cultures believed otherwise, hence the Viking graves and pyramids full of treasure). Squirrelling stuff away in the face of our own transience is an expression of the human hope of immortality. It is one way of understanding the line from TS Eliot's "The Waste Land", "these fragments I have shored against my ruins", which acknowledges both the impulse to hold on and its futility.

The urge to have more is tied to the will to live. Consciously or otherwise, the clothing industry is selling us fragments to shore against our ruins.

Michael

It is something of an understatement to say that my father was not interested in clothes. He would complain if he had to wear a tie and he referred to Marks & Spencer as "my tailor". As soon as he retired, he gave all his suits to charity and swore he'd never wear one again. And yet it was he who taught me two of the most important lessons about clothes.

I was in my early teens, experimenting with my wardrobe and anxiously proud of my new flared trousers, which were – it pains me to write – light brown and so synthetic that they had a slight sheen to them. My father's drainpipe jeans seemed offensively wrong to me and I felt self-conscious about them in the way only an adolescent can – as if his outmoded-ness somehow reflected on me. I tried every trick I could think of to persuade him to buy some flares of his own. He laughed. "I'm going to keep wearing these," he said, "and if I wait long enough they'll be in fashion again."

He was right, of course, but I couldn't see that until much later, until I'd seen flares come and go, come and go from my desk in the offices of *Vogue*, like an inevitable tide. Teenagers are seeing trends for the first time, so the cyclical nature of fashion is not yet obvious to them – one reason why it is so ruthlessly marketed at the young.

When I picture my father, he is wearing his workshop clothes: trousers, shirts and jumpers that were spattered in paint, blotched by bleach, gummed with glue and stained with oil, whose rips and tears he'd healed with duct tape. He was an engineer, always fixing things and doing DIY, mending a neighbour's gate or making someone a new letterbox, unblocking someone's drain or turning something on his wood lathe. I treasure a little needle case he made me and some trays made of ash wood (he wrote "ash tray" on the underside in his barely legible cursive). To this day the smell of sawdust makes me happy. He could make furniture, too, and at his funeral, when we spoke about his life, my siblings and I stood at a simple oak lectern he had made for the church after the original one, carved in the shape of an eagle, was stolen. He was creative and could make beautiful things. He just didn't care about wearing them.

Everyone needs clothes for getting messy in – that is the second lesson my father taught me. Not just clothes that don't matter, but ones whose very purpose is not-mattering. If you don't have any, keep some back next time you have a clear-out and be sure to make a mess in them.

My father demonstrated to the teenage me that there are times when clothes are inhibiting and get in the way. To be completely in the flow of creating, of making something with your hands, is an act of forgetting the self. And what the self is wearing.

Needing to belong

You know that dream where you turn up to a job interview or something really important and you're completely naked? It shines a light on our fundamental need to belong and on the role of clothes in achieving this (our survival chances are better in a group, remember). Tribal dress is an outward expression of social cooperation and our fear of wearing the "wrong" clothes is the fear of not being accepted by the group.

Even today, when fashion in the developed world has never been more plural and "anything goes", an alien arriving from another planet would be able to spot patterns and conformity in what we wear just as clearly as we can detect the sartorial markings of Hell's Angels or Moonies or Arsenal fans. We may not do it consciously but, like it or not, we're all wearing tribal costume.

It may be innate to want to fit in, but the specifics of how we do so are learned. Peer pressure kicks in hard in the teenage years, when we start to dress ourselves and search for a non-familial tribe, but it's present throughout our lives. Witness Jane Austen, a reluctant participant in the social follies of her peers who wrote that to have tidy hair "was all [her] ambition": even she bowed to social pressure and wore her "aunt's gown and handkerchief" when the occasion demanded it. Courtiers at the country estates of Louis XV and Madame de Pompadour were provided with outfits to wear – a different colour for each estate – and it would have been social death not to put them on. Even today, following fashion is a herd activity: the truly original dresser is a rare creature.

Those who do choose to turn their backs on the pursuit of sartorial belonging inevitably end up defining themselves as part of another tribe through their adopted dress. Take a look at monks and nuns, hippies and tree-huggers. Mahatma Gandhi, a Western-educated lawyer, wore a dhoti and shawl to align himself with the tribe of the poor and underprivileged he dedicated his life to helping. Even naturists, in their complete rejection of clothing, look like a tribe in their communal nakedness. There's no escape: opting out itself becomes a tribal statement in the fluent Esperanto of getting dressed.

And yet... as well as the need to belong we also harbour a desire to feel special, which is heightened in post-Enlightenment Western culture with its humanist emphasis on the individual. It's more than the evolutionary need to attract a mate and dressing for status: it is the desire to express our personality and our uniqueness through the choices we make. It's about that particular constellation of jewellery, clothing, hairstyle, footwear and accessories that is unmistakably "you" and no one else, as singular as a fingerprint. If you don't believe you have a personal style, try making yourself buy the first thing you see when you walk into a shop.

I hope that by now you're starting to appreciate the number and the power of the forces that jostle and tussle inside our craniums when we stand before the wardrobe wondering what to wear. One reason we can feel so hopeless and paralysed in that moment is that we are being pulled in opposite directions by these two conflicting impulses: the need to belong and the wish to stand out – the desire to express both our uniqueness and our acceptability at the same time.

It's no wonder we feel torn.

Them and us

Another problem with belonging is that not everyone can belong; tribes define themselves by othering. Unpleasant truths about human nature start to appear when you deconstruct the meaning of clothes, in particular the ugly ways in which clothing has been used throughout history to ostracise, control and oppress people. Forcing Jewish people to wear yellow armbands in Nazi Germany was the first step on the road to the concentration camps, where their clothes were taken away from them: the first step towards mass murder. Belonging and exclusion are two sides of the same coin.

History is punctuated by the attempts of the powerful to reinforce the pecking order by making laws to restrict what others could wear. So-called sumptuary laws (from the Latin *sumptus*, meaning "expenditure", the same root as "sumptuous") were designed both to control spending on luxuries and to stop the poor dressing like the rich. Such laws cropped up all over the globe, sometimes purporting to be economic measures, like the 1571 Act of Parliament in Britain designed to stimulate domestic wool consumption. It decreed that on Sundays and holidays, all males over six years of age, except for the nobility and "persons of degree", were to wear woollen caps on pain of a fine of three farthings per day; its legacy is the flat cap that became a symbol of the English working classes. The Act was repealed after 26 years, and eventually the flat cap became part of the leisure wear of aristocrats (think of Prince Philip out shooting).

Even when sumptuary laws were ostensibly about boosting domestic industry or preserving public morals, in practice they always had the effect of keeping people in their station. Shakespeare understood the correlation between dress and social standing: the "vaulting ambition" that makes Macbeth murder his way to power means he dresses in "borrowed robes", and the title he snatches "hangs loose about him, like a giant's robe upon a dwarfish thief".

As the French philosopher Michel de Montaigne pointed out in his 1580 essay "On Sumptuary Laws", rules about who could wear what simply made the forbidden fruit more appetising. He argued that telling people they couldn't wear things like velvet and gold lace brought those objects "into a greater esteem" and "set everyone more agog to… wear them". The true way to put people off such things, he said, "would be to beget in men a contempt of silks and gold as vain, frivolous and useless". Instead, the banned items became aspirational, so sumptuary laws never worked for long. But that didn't stop people making them.

The Ancient Greeks decreed that the lower classes

could not appear in dyed clothes in public places such as the theatre, while the Romans had strict laws about who could wear purple – an expensive dye that was made by boiling sea snails in lead vats for days, a foul-smelling process. It took over 9,000 snails to make a single gram of dye, and the third-century emperor Aurelian supposedly wouldn't let his wife buy a purple shawl because it literally cost its weight in gold. In the following century, the sumptuary laws were tightened so that only the emperor himself was allowed to wear purple and the colour became linked forever to the ruling class, hence the expression "born to the purple".

You might have guessed that the Tudors would be great enthusiasts for sumptuary laws. Cloth of gold had long been considered the material of the monarchy in England, and Henry VII enshrined in law that it could be used only by the king's family and the very highest members of the nobility. His son, Henry VIII, passed numerous Acts of Apparel throughout his lifetime, largely to keep the emergent merchant class in their place and to separate them at a glance from the nobility. In the first parliament of his reign in 1510, "An Act agaynst wearing of costly Apparell" went into a level of detail that today seems comical: "Velvet of crimson or blue is prohibited to anyone under the degree of a knight of the garter; no person under a knight (excepting sons of lords, judges, those of the king's council, and the mayor of London) is to wear velvet in his gown and doublet, or satin or damask in his gown or coat."

His daughters Mary and Elizabeth followed suit, with

Elizabeth I issuing a series of proclamations against "excess of apparel" that did not shrink from specifics: a baron's eldest son's wife could wear gold or silver lace, for instance. She is said to have sent written reprimands to courtiers whose ruffs threatened to compete in height or fullness with her own. Those magnificent portraits of Tudor monarchs decked out in their finery and dripping with jewels were not family snaps: they were the tools of propaganda and power.

When the making of sumptuary laws died out, the unwritten law of social convention took over. Social order was still expressed through dress but it was maintained by the pressure of the group and the attendant fear of being cast out of it: by etiquette rather than edict. The clearest illustration of this is the Victorians' set of rules about mourning dress, which were as detailed and petty as anything the Tudors had devised. Queen Victoria, grieving the loss of her husband Albert, did not need to make actual laws because the socially ambitious – in other words, almost everyone with the means to afford it – willingly followed her lead and donned head-to-toe black accessorised with black jet jewellery.

There were manuals you could consult about precisely what to wear if, say, your second cousin died, and for how long you should wear it. Widows were expected to wear full mourning for two years, but if your uncle or aunt died just two months would do – never mind that you might have loathed your husband and been devoted to your mother's sister. Shops such as Jay's of Regent Street in London dedicated themselves to the lucrative business of mourning dress. As usual, it was the women who were most put upon by this trend – their entire outfits changed, whereas men just wore their usual dark suits and added black ties, hatbands and gloves. Wearing black had long been an expression of grief and loss, but this extreme craze for mourning dress worked like any other fashion trend. Of course you could ignore the rules, but if you wanted to belong you toed the line.

The single person most responsible for wresting the dictates of fashion from the grasp of upper class ladies in corsets and heirloom jewellery was Coco Chanel. Born into poverty, she seized the opportunity presented by the rise of the middle classes and the social destruction of the First World War. She made paste jewellery fashionable and designed clothes that allowed women to be more active and comfortable than they had been for generations. It's one of the great ironies of fashion history that the name of the woman who played a key role in democratising fashion has become a luxury brand that sells dresses for the price of a car. It's also a telling comment on the business of fashion itself: even something revolutionary, given time, becomes establishment and exclusive.

The idea of exclusion is hard-baked into the concept of fashion. The word "exclusive" – which our culture abhors in the context of race or gender – is freely used to market aspirational products. Not every company goes as far as US teen brand Abercrombie & Fitch did at the beginning of this century, though: with its image of sexy, preppy, WASP-y types, exclusion was the very root of its success. It transpired that this image extended to its employment practices – their "look policy" meant that white employees were the ones visible on the shop floor, while others were confined to the stockroom. Eventually, the company was hit with class-action lawsuits for discrimination, settling out of court for US$40 million in 2004.

Like the need to belong, exclusion is part of the hierarchical social structure humans have created for themselves, and fashion makes this exclusion visible. That's the ugly truth. If you're in any doubt, take a look at a gang of teenagers eyeing up each other's trainers, and put yourself in the shoes (so to speak) of the one who can't afford the cool brands. Tribal dressing articulates the primal, existential fear of being left out, which is, ultimately, the fear of not surviving, the fear of death.

When it is no longer exclusive, fashion moves on. It wasn't the sheer absurdity of long pointy shoes or crinolines that made them fall from favour: it was the fact that servants started wearing them.

The dictates of fashion

There is a moment when, in our heads, the deal is done. We decide to buy. We may have been searching for that particular piece of clothing for months, or it may be a spontaneous love-at-first-sight thing. Either way, we are heading for the till and reaching for our wallets. What made us want this particular dress – or jumper or skirt – but feel completely indifferent to the one next to it? How do we choose what to buy?

Trying to pin down what influences us is like looking for hay in a haystack: influence is everywhere. And when enough whims, sparks, nudges and triggers converge in our heads, they make the synapses fire along the neural pathway that leads us to Pay Now. One reason influence is hard to pin down is that we inhale it all our lives. We breathe it in from our families, our education, our nationalities – and it's invisible as air because we are inside it. Then there's the visible stuff, the smoke that's blown into our faces by the modern world: from images of celebrities who have teams of people working on that look, to friends on social media who don't.

In addition, each item in our wardrobes, every look we adopt, comes with a historical hinterland of associations that makes it speak to us. A simple white T-shirt might carry associations of James Dean, school PE lessons, Karl Lagerfeld's 1991 collection when it was worn under Chanel's signature tweed, summer at the beach… it will be a different cocktail for each of us. A military-look jacket isn't only attractive because army style is having a fashion moment. It comes trailing clouds of stories: for me these include Goya's portrait of the Duke of Wellington, the *Sgt Pepper* album cover, a photo my father in uniform, my brother's toy soldiers, a childhood trip to see *The Nutcracker*…

Into that swirling mix are added generous dollops of advertising, marketing and brand-positioning, which subtly interact with our own ideas of what we think suits us and our sense of how we'd like to be seen. And all of that is happening in a nanosecond, drawing us magnetically towards this jacket or those trousers, way before such practical considerations as fit and feel and size and comfort get a look-in. And anyway, such practical matters can be trampled beneath the thundering hooves of influence: who hasn't bought a dress that is too see-through, trousers that are too tight or a jumper that's itchy and chosen to ignore that inconvenient fact?

Trend forecasters (yes, it's an actual job) spend their time sniffing the breeze to see what will be the Next Big Thing. They look at macro-trends (big global shifts) based on what is happening in the world of art, architecture and economy, and also on how consumers are feeling. And they look at other, more immediate trends which bubble up from what is happening on the street, in underground cultures, in music and online. When these so-called cool hunters spot a colour, a fabric, a key item or a silhouette and they see it happening in several places, they pass it on to their clients in the fashion and design industry. And – fast-forward a bit – there it is in the shops, trying to worm its way into our wardrobes.

It's easy to feel that we are passive victims standing before the tidal wave that is fashion today. We have the impression that fashion is imposed upon us, which is why people talk about "the dictates of fashion". In fact, the relationship between catwalk and sidewalk is more subtle. It's more like rain, evaporating from the ground and later falling back down on us, round and round in an endless circle. Fashion picks up on what's already in the wind and gives it form as clothing. It's a giant feedback loop, an amplifier and an embodiment – with a slight built-in delay – of what we already feel. We just may not know it quite yet.

It's telling that the overarching trends of the 21st century – "athleisure" and vintage clothing – are, in their essence, what ordinary people have worn for most of history: comfortable clothes you can move in and hand-me-downs. It would be good news for us and for the planet if we could just stay with this return to relative sanity. But inevitably fashion has made expensive versions of these trends and will, ultimately, need to move us on again.

The thing about influence is that it's a shape-shifter,

constantly updating itself and able to flow through the smallest of cracks. Even someone raised in the forest by wolves will, given time in the right environment, end up wanting the same pair of jeans as everyone else.

Reason for return

The wardrobe with no mistakes in it is a unicorn-rare creature. There are myriad reasons we buy clothes we don't wear much (or ever) and ridiculous, uncomfortable shoes. Some of these reasons have nothing to do with taste or personal style or our deepest fears: some are just tediously practical, like sizing, which varies from brand to brand and country to country to the point where the numbers on the labels become meaningless.

Some reasons for mistakes, though, are in our heads. "When I shop I forget who I am," a friend tells me. "I forget what my life is like." Shopping for a fantasy version of our lives is exactly what the brands try to persuade us to do. That dress might look perfect in the advert for romping through the Californian surf, but if you holiday in the Hebrides it may not prove quite so useful. Even if we do remember that clothes might need to have an actual role in our real lives, there is likely to be a helpful shop assistant on hand to reassure us that "you can dress it up or down!" and telling you it's the last one in that size. When I was younger – I'm not proud of this – I occasionally bought something just because the shop assistant was incredibly pressing and I just couldn't work out how to say no...

When you buy the wrong thing online, saying no is easy and returns may be free to make it even easier. But they still require lots of parcel tape and a trip to the post office. And it's raining. So maybe we'll keep it just in case… If we do get round to returning it, the reasons we can choose from are things like "too big", "too small", "not as described" and "wrong item sent". They don't start to approach the reality of the situation. Here's a more honest list of "reasons for return":

- dopamine surge
- purchased while bored/hungry/tired/hormonal
- comfort shopping
- it was in the sale
- it was in the second markdown of the sale
- it looked good on someone I know
- the model is much taller than me
- it seems to be made of plastic
- no one on this planet is that shape
- already have something almost exactly the same
- had a favourite dress that colour when I was 10
- thought I was someone else
- felt I had nothing to wear
- panicked about the planet
- all of the above

Will it kill a dolphin?

As oxymorons go, "sustainable fashion" is right up there with "comfortable heels" and "flattering anorak". Sustainable means something that lasts, and fashion, by its very nature, does not. It does precisely the opposite because it is, as we've seen, about novelty and change and therefore by definition not sustainable. A piece of clothing can be more or less sustainable. But fashion itself? Never.

Now we've cleared that up, let's stand together in front of the wardrobe again, this time with our save-the-planet specs on. Perhaps we'd better sit down.

We'll start with that little black dress – is it environmentally friendly? What is its carbon footprint and could it have been made by workers in a sweatshop? Were they fairly paid or could they be living in slavery or forced-labour camps? How much polluted water did that T-shirt create and how many microfibres will those joggers release into the water system and then the ocean? Will they kill a dolphin? Come to mention it, what are the living conditions of the animals this cashmere jumper came from? Which is the greenest fabric, anyway – is viscose really better for the planet than cotton? What about all those chemicals used to process the plant fibres? The label says "made in England", but where did the materials come from originally? I should probably wash those jeans, but wouldn't it be greener not to? And if I wash them, which detergent should I use? Should I use one that comes as a sheet rather than a liquid to save transport costs? Some people don't have any shoes, so why on earth do I have so many? I think I'm starting to hyperventilate: please can I have a cup of tea?

The full answers to these questions – except the cup-of-tea one (the answer's yes) – are hard to pin down and they trowel on another thick layer of guilt to the business of getting dressed. What we know for certain is that, just when it seemed the world was going to end in a welter of pointless consumerism, with waiting lists for £10,000 handbags and dresses for the price of a sandwich, climate change came along to bring us to our senses before it's too late. Which it may be already, for human beings at least – although rats and cockroaches will apparently be fine.

Set aside for a moment methane from cows and pollution from cars: the fashion industry accounts for about 10% of global carbon emissions and 20% of industrial waste water. It uses more energy than international flights and shipping combined. The UN estimates that the making of a single pair of jeans uses 7,500 – 10,000 litres of water, which is the amount the average person drinks in 10 years, and every year nearly 70 million barrels of oil are used to make polyester. In Chile, there is a mountain of discarded clothes that is visible from space. I could go on but I'm sure you get the picture. You probably had the picture already, but it's tempting to turn it round to face the wall. I'm not judging – I'm as guilty as the next person of doing just that: swearing off fast fashion but allowing myself just one more hit because that particular thing is exactly what's missing from my wardrobe.

The vast scale of the fast-fashion industry is the polar opposite of how clothing used to be made. Once upon a time, your neighbour in the village spun wool from the sheep you saw every day in the fields, someone else you knew wove it into cloth and the local dressmaker turned it into a dress for you. You could probably see the entire process from your front door.

Today the supply chains of Big Fashion are so long and convoluted that checking every link for sustainability and human rights abuses is virtually impossible, even if the will to do so is there. Plus it's hard to keep up: not long ago, synthetic fleece was good news because it could be made out of recycled bottles, but now it's nasty and evil (and not just because after a couple of washes it tries to change back into a plastic bottle). It's much easier to take the eco-glasses off and lose them down the back of the sofa with all the others.

We do need a certain number of clothes, but not nearly as many as we have. And we have to perform an athletic piece of cognitive dissonance to carry on living in a consumer society while knowing it may be a kind of slow species suicide. We do our bit with recycling, handing things over to charity shops and perhaps choosing not to buy another white T-shirt, but our efforts seem pathetically small while war is raging and the rainforest is being torn down.

Aren't we just salving our consciences while Doomsday approaches inexorably, beyond our control? Sometimes it's hard not to feel defeated and impotent. And yes, quite depressed.

Maybe a spot of shopping would cheer us up?

Consuming passion

As I walked down Oxford Street recently, I saw the words "WE'VE GOT TO CHANGE" in gigantic letters on the facade of a famous department store. So far, so good. But when I turned the corner, I read the rest of the sentence on the side of the building: "THE WAY WE SHOP". Hmm. The reality is that we've got to change not the way we shop but the fact that we shop, much as the big stores desperately need it to be otherwise.

In the same way, in the "buy less, buy better" mantra of the anti-fast-fashion campaign, the key word is "buy": the fact that we will keep shopping is implicit. A somewhat greener mantra would be "buy second hand", or better still, "borrow, swap, lend". But you're unlikely to see that on a magazine cover or in two-metre-high letters on a shopfront. And while we're looking at catchphrases, why do we say "junk food" but not "junk fashion"? Both are, ultimately, bad for us.

Some fast-fashion retailers have launched "conscious collections", using recycled or organic materials. But what about the carbon footprint of the entire company: how do we know this is anything more than a bit of reputation-offsetting? Some shops provide bins for you to recycle clothes (once you're already on their premises). Clothes may be labelled "planet friendly" or "sustainable". But because we've learned to be cynical and alert to greenwashing and "woke capitalism", these efforts raise as many questions as they answer. We suspect we're being manipulated and can't prove that we're not.

Small "slow-fashion" companies are emerging, offering fewer pieces a year and a lower environmental impact, although not everyone can or wants to pay for them. There has been growth in sales of second-hand clothing and shops where you can rent items for a few days for a special occasion. There are even virtual fashions that you can buy to "wear" for social media purposes, without a real stitch in them. But these changes just repackage the problem without actually tackling it at the root, which is not sustainability but overconsumption and the urges that drive it. And that's a hard one to fix when the full wardrobe seems empty and we are encouraged to reinvent ourselves by shopping.

Not so long ago, a couple of hooks on the back of a door was all most people needed by way of storage solutions for their clothes. Or maybe a wooden chest if you were lucky. A wardrobe (from the French *garde-robe*, literally "keep-dress") was a room where royalty and the nobility kept their clothes (it also meant privy or toilet for a while). Even when the word came to mean the piece of furniture we know today, it was still for the prosperous. Manual workers would have had one or two sets of clothes and a Sunday best outfit.

How, then, did we get to where we are today, with so much stuff in our lives – and in our wardrobes in particular? The answer, in three words, is the industrial revolution. Without it, the relationship between humans and the natural world would probably have been sustainable. But once a giant tree could be ripped out of the earth in seconds, once factories could spew out literally acres of fabric in a day, the fine equilibrium between man and nature was trampled in the dust.

The mass production of the machine age meant that, for the first time, supply outstripped demand and we had to be persuaded to buy stuff that we didn't actually need. Advertising and marketing industries mushroomed into life to do the persuading. Their words and images fell on fertile ground because, as we've already seen, our brains are fascinated by novelty and possessions are a kind of proxy for living. The notion of buying things because we actually need them got buried beneath the demands of commerce, and consumerism was born.

Consumer culture encourages us to indulge ourselves in order to feel better: owning more new stuff is conflated with happiness; objects and emotions become surrogates for each other, infinitely entangled. Perhaps as a side effect of this, shopping has become a recreational and social habit, something to do with friends for fun. Just like going to a restaurant and eating too much.

The philosopher Immanuel Kant would have argued against such behaviour: his idea of the "categorial imperative" stated that you should only do something if it would be fine for everyone else to do so too. If the whole world consumed clothing as we do in the West, the planet simply could not support it. It's been estimated that buying a maximum of eight new items a year could reduce fashion's emissions by 37% in the world's major cities.

What should we hope for? Health warnings on clothes? That the cachet of having new things itself goes out of fashion? It could happen – by 2025 the total value of resold and thrifted clothing is predicted to climb to US$77bn a year, outstripping the growth in fast fashion, which is predicted to be US$40bn. We can hope that humankind will finally see that it exists within a fragile ecosystem and does not have dominion over it – already a river in New Zealand has been granted legal personhood, with the rights of a human.

All our efforts to recycle, putting empty yoghurt pots and bits of silver foil in a bin under the sink, may feel futile but at least they're rewiring our minds: every time we flatten a cardboard box or a plastic bottle a neural pathway is strengthened, and it forces us to take a long, hard look at packaging. It is not such a great leap to take a long, hard look at how we package ourselves.

Do our bodies need so many wrappings?

New to you

In the guilt section of the wardrobe, second-hand clothes occupy a smaller space than new ones – they're T-shirts rather than coats, as it were. While they still feed our craving for novelty, they satisfy it in a lower-impact way. I've bought second-hand clothes since I was a teenager rummaging in jumble sales in the village hall for satiny undergarments to wear as dresses. It used to be something you were expected to grow out of – a student habit, born of necessity. But today second hand is booming, facilitated by technology, which puts jumble sales and auctions literally in your pocket. It's partly a response to the planetary crisis and partly a backlash against the boring homogeneity of mass-produced fashion.

Also booming is the number of words for second hand: pre-loved, pre-owned, reused, recycled, upcycled, repurposed, new-to-you, thrift dressing… The fact that so many euphemisms have been found to avoid saying "second hand" tells it's own story: used clothes have unpleasant associations for anyone who grew up in poverty or in wartime. Even in an era when recycling and reusing are meant to save us all, second-hand clothing still has something of an image problem – not least because, as we've seen, the ability to afford new things speaks of status and hence of survival. I know several people who have an almost pathological resistance to it. They find it unhygienic or cite the smell – of mustiness or mothballs, of "old people". Or maybe it's the scent of others; clothing is personal, after all. It would be more accurate to say "second body" rather than second hand. But perhaps that would be too much reality.

Second-hand dressing is just a return to how things used to be. For most of history, clothes were hand-made and handed on. Catherine Parr, shoe addict and Henry VIII's final wife, inherited a vast collection of dresses that had belonged to her by-then-headless predecessor, Katherine Howard. History doesn't relate what Parr felt about these hand-me-downs, but the simple fact was that rich gowns were valuable bits of property.

As a matter of routine, clothes used to be "turned" to show the reverse of the fabric when the outside was faded or worn, or made into something else. In 18th-century London, the second-hand clothing industry centred on Seven Dials, but by the 1850s it had moved to the area around Petticoat Lane in the East End, where a roaring wholesale and retail trade took place. Clothes were "translated" or "clobbered" (remade) and dresses were cleaned with turpentine. The Victorian lady of fashion might pass a dress on to her maid, who was just as likely to sell it as to wear it. Clothes were collected door to door and distributed to the poor via charities, and there was a big export trade, particularly in men's clothes.

During the Second World War, you didn't need coupons for clothes that were second hand, and the government ran a "Make Do and Mend" campaign featuring "Mrs Sew-and-Sew". Magazines gave tips on how to make a new coat out of two old ones or a dress from old curtains. The message was "thrift is the fashion". People became resourceful about how they used materials; after the war, parachute silk was used to make lingerie. It was into that frugal climate that Dior's fabric-hungry New Look erupted, which explains why it seemed so shocking (although the look itself was in fact nostalgic in its silhouette and proportions). In the times of relative plenty since the 1960s, second hand has had a different role – avant-garde, arty, counter-cultural. Today, celebrities appear on red carpets in "designer vintage", which is fashion-speak for "second hand but expensive".

It is rare for me nowadays not to be wearing something that has had a former life elsewhere. I'm lucky to live near two good dress agencies where people can sell their designer mistakes, with the shop taking a commission. Or perhaps they are not mistakes, merely last season and therefore in need of replacing. Either way, the agencies' owners are picky – clothes have to be a label they know will sell, in good condition and dry-cleaned. As a customer you get more quality for your money than you would buying new clothes, even in a sale. Items with a label such as Gucci or Prada are the rescue dogs of my wardrobe – rehomed and all the more lovable because they are unwanted by someone else.

As with all second-hand shopping, the dress agency is about serendipity. Either there is something you love that fits you, or there isn't. You don't waste time trawling through rail after rail of the current fashions, convinced there must be something that will suit you, comparing sizes or styles or colours. It's a black-and-white process. The trick is to visit often, and if you happen to arrive just after a rich shopaholic who is the same size as you, you hit the jackpot. Best of all, you sidestep the fleeting tyranny of fashion: whether that dress is this season, last season or many seasons old is not the question; the hype and the chatter fall away and you are left answering the only questions that should matter: does it suit me? Do I feel good in it? Will I use it? Do I love it?

The very questions that the fashion industry hopes you'll forget to ask.

Signs of distress

In the language of clothes, as in any language, it is possible to tell lies. Corsets lie about our waist size, for instance, long fake nails about our nutritional health, tight leggings about our muscle tone and high heels about our stature. As for codpieces... well, you can work that one out by yourself. And in recent years, some clothes, like some of the people wearing them, have started to lie about their age.

Clothing that has been made to look old – as opposed to actually being old – is known as "distressed". That means, according to the dictionary, "to give fabric or furniture the appearance of being older than it is" rather than emotional distress, although of course one can be a sign of the other. The trend for old-looking clothes probably has its roots in utility wear, in particular denim jeans which became more comfortable when they were broken in. In the 1970s, worn jeans looked hippie-cool and anti-establishment – people wore them in the bath and scrubbed them to soften them up and age them. Later, lycra and factory stone-washing came along to simulate wear and tear, while the aesthetic residue of the punk and grunge fashion moments filtered into the mainstream.

In the 21st century, sartorial distress seems to be here to stay. Even when it's not all over the catwalk, it flourishes at street level: frayed hems, pre-scuffed shoes, suede with already-bald patches and jeans with holes in. Sometimes these holes are so big that the jeans are barely attached at the knees. In Japan, for an extra frisson of wildness, a company made jeans out of scratched and torn denim that had first been given to lions and tigers to maul. Mainstream brands such as J Crew and Diesel sold trousers ready-spattered with paint, and as I write dirty-looking new trainers are all the rage. Anyone on a smaller budget – or simply alive to the irony of paying a premium for worn-looking clothes – can turn to the internet, which is awash with advice on how to age them yourself: just stock up on razor blades, bleach and sandpaper, and off you go.

You might wonder what all this deliberate shabbiness means. I certainly did, especially after I bought a pair of washed-out, ripped jeans in a down-with-the-kids moment which I'll pretend was research. The first thing I noticed when I put them on was that I felt relaxed and off-duty. I felt properly casual, rather than I'm-wearing-casual-clothes casual. Perhaps that is one function of beaten-up clothes: their deliberate un-smartness states that you are opting out of the polished look, removing some of the pressure placed on us by all that glossy consumer marketing (although ripped jeans also get marketed). I'm not playing that game, these jeans say: I don't want to try that hard. Though not trying hard requires a certain effort – when it comes to distressed clothing, the ironies pile up like ironing on a bad laundry day.

For most of history, clothes that looked old (rather than just being old, which was normal) were an indication of poverty: people who could afford opulent clothing wore it as a badge of superiority and power. Today's down-at-heel look is the modern version of Marie Antoinette's shepherdess costume and equally inauthentic. The difference is that it is now adopted by the masses, possibly while they eat their cake.

The studiously unkempt hippies, the rips and safety pins of punk, the ratty grunge moment of the early '90s – these were counter-cultural choices, protests against the status quo, born in an age that had the luxury of options. Today's wave of distressing might also be part protest: against mass-production and the sickening acres of new clothes, which devalue the emotional power of novelty. Although (irony alert!) the distressed look is often mass-produced itself.

In the 21st century, we are living – in the West, at least – in a time of material oversupply, and that is the context to which fashion is reacting. Because that is what fashion – protean, evanescent and sinuous as a snake – is always doing: twisting and turning and reinventing itself against both its current context and its historical hinterland. It is often a contrary beast: plumpness and paleness were prized when thinness signified malnutrition and a tan meant you worked outdoors. So it follows that, in a time of extreme plenty, it is fashionable to appear deprived.

But that's not the whole story. The state of the planet, in both climatic and humanitarian terms, adds another, complicating layer to the expression of status through clothes: what has come to be known as virtue signalling. It is not enough to convey success; we have to convey goodness and maybe humility too. Worn-looking clothing may be the consumerist version of sackcloth and ashes. It trumps second-hand, rented or borrowed clothing because you can read it at a glance; you don't need to be told of its hidden virtue.

In the trend for distressed clothing, we can read a critical commentary on modern life, with its materialism and homogeneity and human-centredness. It seems to be saying that what is on offer is no longer worthy of aspiration. Distressed clothes are a kind of refusal, the sartorial equivalent of self-harm. It is hard not to discern in them a post-apocalyptic subtext: is it a foretaste of how we'll be dressing when we've used up the Earth's resources, if our species is still here?

The fig leaf

Clothing has, in the foundational myths of Western culture, been linked from the start to lies, deceit and betrayal. Exhibit A: the story of Adam and Eve and the expulsion from the Garden of Eden.

The Fall has been interpreted in many ways – and I'm going to take a risk here and assume you don't think it's a literal account. The most superficial reading introduces a punitive male creator and lays the foundation stone of the patriarchy by establishing woman's inferiority to man and then blaming her for letting evil into paradise. If you dig a bit deeper, the Tree of Knowledge could represent what is called the cognitive revolution – the massive change in the brain of our species that occurred about 70,000 years ago and sets us apart from other great apes; in other words, it might stand for the beginnings of human consciousness. The Fall might also represent the birth of language – the very means of storytelling itself – because with the first utterance came also the potential to lie.

What is not up for debate, however, is that the Fall concerns clothes: the first thing Adam and Eve do after a significant telling-off from God is slap a fig leaf over their genitals. Or that is how we picture it today; in fact, chapter 3 of Genesis says that God made them "garments of skins" – the fig leaf was a later invention. You might point out that covering up our nakedness had a practical purpose – protecting us from injury – but it would be limiting to see the story of Adam and Eve as a tale about the origins of workwear. The social function of clothes – in organising, classifying and imposing order on humans living together in groups – has its genesis here. Many anthropologists hold that the chief function of religion is to control reproduction; if they are right, to have everyone wandering around naked is not an obvious first step to that end.

In Hebrew, the language of the Old Testament, the root of the word for clothes (*beged*) is the same as the one for "deceit" and "betrayal", and the root of the word for "coat" is the same as the one for "embezzlement". In the 13th century, Rumi, the Persian poet and Sufi mystic, recognised this connection between clothing and dishonesty when he wrote that "a truth can walk naked, but a lie always needs to be dressed". And even in modern English, words such as "cloak" and "fabricate" point to the inherent deception of covering up (there goes another one).

Clothes weave a fiction around us, and we use this deceptive power when we get dressed, hiding bits of our bodies we don't feel confident about (hence my legions of black trousers) and drawing attention to other bits that we judge acceptable. I once shared an office with

Isabella Blow, the fashion editor and muse known for her outlandish and eye-catching way of dressing, who died by her own hand in 2007. She told me that she dressed that way because she was ugly: she wanted people to notice her clothes and not her. Beneath her extravagant plumage, she was trying to make her physical self invisible.

All clothing is artifice – Issy's wardrobe was just an extreme example. If the animal kingdom is any guide, some washing and a spot of grooming for nits is about all that's natural. And yet body shame in the human species is so culturally ingrained that public nakedness was long considered a sign of madness. It was such a transgression of societal norms that it could be used as a form of protest: witness Lady Godiva on her legendary anti-taxation ride in the 11th century and climate change activists today.

For a lot of women, the prospect of a beach holiday is like getting an invitation to a party and then seeing that it says "dress code: bra and pants". Had we been alive two centuries ago, we would have "bathed" in voluminous, bloomered and skirted costumes and – wait for it – stockings. It must have been like swimming in seaweed, so surely we should be counting our blessings that we now live in a culture that lets us go near-naked and feel the delicious lap of water against our bare skin? That's hard to do, though, when the media persists in weaponising shame, exhorting us to Get Bikini-Ready in Just Six Weeks and ridiculing celebrities who fail to hold their tummies in.

The story of Eve makes it clear that clothing is part of a curse – for both men and women (although, in a three-for-one deal, women also get second-class citizenship and pain in childbirth). In the myths of the Judaeo-Christian tradition, our preoccupation with clothes is an integral part of our flawed humanity.

We were cast out of paradise into the shopping mall.

It's a man's world

When children first go to school, if they are asked to draw a scientist they draw roughly equal numbers of men and women. By the time they are seven or eight years old, they draw more men than women, and by the age of 14 they draw four times as many men: cultural bias trickles in as we grow up. And it is being amplified in artificial intelligence, which is mostly designed by men and knows only what has gone before.

There is debate about whether the patriarchal structure of society is natural, born out of genetic differences between males and females, or whether it is imposed as part of a male-dominated system of power. The answer could be a bit of both – the genetic differences could cause the domination, for instance – although experiments such as the draw-a-scientist test suggest that it is learned as much as inborn. What is not up for debate is that we still live in a world designed for men. That's a world where women are 17% more likely than men to die in a car crash, where women are interrupted more than men in conversation, where women are 2.5 times more likely than men to be on anti-depressants and where there are five times as many studies on erectile dysfunction as there are on pre-menstrual syndrome.

How did it come to this? There is debate, too, about the origins of patriarchy, but I'll briefly outline what I find the most plausible scenario, because it has a great effect on what women wear. And if you don't agree with the specifics, let's just agree that it exists: we can reread history all we like, but we can't rewrite it.

It's likely that hunter-gatherer societies were more or less egalitarian, or possibly even female-centric, since females gave birth to the next generation and ensured continuity in a way that males, biologically, could not (the concept of fatherhood may not even have existed at that time). Recent research suggests that females went out hunting, although menstruation, pregnancy and child-rearing must have been easier to manage if you didn't also have to go out spearing things – perhaps they got a few years of maternity leave.

Once people stopped being nomadic and started to lead settled, agricultural lives, they acquired property and chattels and needed to manage food supplies. This meant that family, blood lines and inheritance became more important. Males needed to know who their children were in order to know who to feed and who was entitled to inherit property, and in order to know this they had to control women, and – crucially – their reproduction. This idea, that it was the shift to agriculture that gave birth to the patriarchal system, is supported by the so-called plough hypothesis, which suggests that societies using ploughs to till the land developed a more gender-based division of labour, because of the physical strength required.

The Old Testament documents this societal shift – hence all that begetting, the endless lists of who fathered whom to shore up the system of male dominance. The story of Jacob and Esau can be read as an allegory of it: Esau, the hairy hunter, is supplanted by Jacob, the smooth-skinned farmer, in a piece of deceit that involved, you guessed it, clothes. Jacob dresses up as his slightly older twin and covers his hands with goat skin to trick his blind, dying father into making him his heir – a cunning plot devised by their mother, of course. Eve is just the first in a long line of Biblical women whose role is largely to take the blame for things, while the men are often suspiciously passive: they are simply obeying God, who ventriloquises the patriarchy for them and just happens to make lots of rules in their favour. All of which answers the question that Gloria Steinem so memorably asked: "Why does God look suspiciously like the ruling class?"

Whether or not you are religious, if you've grown up in the Western world, you've grown up in a society formed in the Judaeo-Christian tradition, which – like other major religions – is patriarchal. This is a tradition whose foundational myth states that woman was created to be man's helpmeet and in which the marriage service, until recently, required the female to promise to obey the male. Marriage was for centuries a worldly matter: a transfer-of-goods ceremony in which the woman is a piece of property handed from one man (her father) to another (her husband). In many cultures, she was – and in Orthodox Judaism, for instance, still is – required to dress differently thereafter. The word "matrimony" spells out her reproductive role, deriving as it does from the Latin word for "mother".

The word chattels, meaning goods or property, shares the same Latin root as the word for cattle. In Old Testament times, to own cattle was a sign of prosperity, which is why my name – Rebecca (Rivka in the Bible) – derives from the word for "heifer". That is not something the baby-naming books tell you, but it was an aspirational name, the Tiffany or Chelsea of its day. Women, not just those named after cows, were chattels – for most of history they had no rights and rape counted as a property violation – and steps had to be taken to keep them secure, as with all property. You didn't want someone to steal your women, nor did you want them to run off of their own accord. So you kept them fenced in and you made sure they weren't too attractive to other men, or that other men didn't set eyes on them. Women, as property in the patriarchal system, were physically confined by men and what they wore was determined by men. Clothes became a tool of the patriarchy, a means of controlling women.

The pioneering fashion historian, James Laver, noted in 1968 that in "patriarchal periods the clothes of the two sexes are as clearly differentiated as possible". I could point out that the entire history of Western dress has taken place in a patriarchal period, but I think what he means is that the differences are exaggerated at times when keeping women under control is most explicit.

Women's clothes didn't just subjugate women; part of their job was to make men feel more manly by contrast. In the Victorian era, as mentioned earlier, the triangle of the female silhouette was the inverse of the male one, and a century later, when men wanted their jobs back after the war and were trying to usher women back into the home, big skirts – those symbols of fertility that exaggerate the hips – popped up once again.

It should follow, therefore, that the increase in unisex clothing today is a sign of the patriarchy breaking down. But imagine if the patriarchy had never existed: the contents of our wardrobes would be very different indeed.

Garments of mass seduction

Just as hostages develop Stockholm syndrome and start identifying with their captors in order to survive, so women had to connive with the patriarchy, stepping into corsets and heels like horses putting their heads into bridles. To this day, our man-pleasing wardrobes exist in the long shadow of this Faustian pact: uncomfortable as it may be for some fashion historians, the bare fact is that for much of history, women have needed a provider, and clothes played their part in securing one.

The Darwinian process of sexual selection, when it takes place in a patriarchal system in which females are disempowered, puts intense pressure on women to attend to their appearance. (It also takes up lots of time which, along with domestic and child-rearing tasks, helps ensure that they don't worry their pretty little heads about men's business.) The twin demands of evolution (the need to attract a mate) and the patriarchy (women as valuable possessions) meant that a tightrope had to be walked. Women had to look attractive yet modest, chaste yet a good reproductive bet, all within the dress codes of their times. Quite a balancing act.

Historically, modesty and chastity were religion-sanctioned virtues designed to ensure that women chose a provider rather than a one-night-stand and potentially a fatherless child. They also ensured that men felt their property – the woman's body, and thus their own descendants – was theirs and no one else's. So-called fallen women were damaged goods, outside society and with reduced survival prospects. Women had a binary choice: Madonna or whore, safe within society or endangered without it. Clothes encoded this distinction: society – and that includes women – decided which clothes lay on which side of the tightrope.

However much flesh a given era permitted a woman to show, there was always the possibility of showing too much of it, or the wrong bits. In the 1920s, the Archbishop of Naples announced that a recent earthquake in Amalfi was caused by God's anger at knee-length skirts, and the state of Utah brought in legislation to fine those who wore in public "skirts higher than three inches above the ankle". In its day, the crespine (a kind of large hairnet that appeared at the end of the 13th century) was deemed immoral because it showed female hair, and for several post-Renaissance centuries, while a revealing décolletage was acceptable, showing the smallest bit of leg was decidedly not.

The V-neck, when it emerged in 1913 after decades of high collars, was considered risky in both moral and medical terms – a top showing a small triangle of skin was dubbed a "pneumonia blouse". Mary Quant, who made the miniskirt fashionable in the 1960s, later recounted how middle-aged businessmen would beat on the shop window shouting: "It's obscene! It's disgusting!" The miniskirt, coinciding as it did with the invention of the contraceptive pill, was synonymous with sexual liberation: it shows perfectly how fluently the language of clothes can articulate a moral shift in society.

The migrating area of flesh that can be shown has been called the Shifting Erogenous Zone, and according to a theory known as the erotic (or the seduction) principle, it's a key driver for changing fashion. This zone supposedly moves around from one part of the female body to another – the bosom, the waist, the legs – in order to renew the erotic appeal to men. The theory itself is a bit out of fashion, probably because the idea that what we wear is to do with attracting a mate is unpalatable today. As a clothes-loving feminist, I find it quite hard to swallow, and there are certainly many other drivers of fashion, but Darwin would probably have loved it. What is certain is that the onus is still on women to keep renewing their appearance: even if we try to ignore it, there is social pressure to vary what we wear and social permission for men to throw on the same thing day after day – Barack Obama always wore the same colour suit to avoid decision fatigue. It is almost impossible to imagine a woman announcing, as my 20-something son did recently, "I did my annual clothes shop last week". For us, decision fatigue comes with the territory.

The unwritten rules about what could and couldn't be worn were enforced by the patriarchy's weapon of choice: shame. Shame is what's known as a social emotion, because it requires an audience, real or imagined (and it is different from guilt, which involves some degree of responsibility). If everyone simply did whatever they wanted, it would be impossible to maintain social order, so shame evolved as a brake to increase the chances of group survival. Just as the function of physical pain is to stop us hurting ourselves, so the function of shame is to stop us damaging our relationships. In other words, shame is social pain.

By stepping outside the patriarchal fence of shame that both protects and corrals them, women risk their wellbeing and even their survival. You may notice I am using the present tense. Slut-shaming, clothes that are "asking for it", looking tarty: these judgements are not routinely passed on men. Even in the most apparently liberal societies, the danger of women's pleasure casts a long and twisted shadow.

It is hard for women to crawl out from under the centuries of cultural baggage and take unchecked pleasure in their bodies and the clothes they put on them. So if you find yourself standing in front of your wardrobe, wondering whether you look too tarty or too frumpy, remember the ancient Madonna/whore quandary. Remember that historically, for a woman to attend to her appearance was a survival skill. A woman got dressed as if her life depended on it. And it pretty much did.

The F–word

Yes. You can be a feminist and still love clothes.

But...

It's difficult to know what being a feminist and loving clothes means for how we dress, because it's hard to strip away all the assumptions that originate with patriarchy. What we want to wear and what the culture we live in wants us to wear are entangled and it is no easy matter to pull them apart. Whatever our gender identity, expressing it takes place against a male-dominant backdrop, and even LGBTQ+ dress has tended to play with tropes of the age-old binary perception of gender, defining itself against the prevailing cultural context even as it seeks its own visual language.

In the book of his seminal 1972 TV series, *Ways of Seeing*, John Berger coined the phrase "the male gaze". This, in essence, is the cultural act of depicting women and the world from the viewpoint of a heterosexual male, and sexually objectifying women. He wrote: "Men act and women appear. Men look at women. Women watch themselves being looked at. This determines not only most relations between men and women but also the relation of women to themselves." Women have lived for so long in a society saturated by the male gaze that we look at other women, and also at ourselves, with it. That pose you strike for a selfie, that pout you put on when you look in the mirror, who is it really for? Much of fashion still enacts the male gaze, offering women as prey to male desires (clothes that stop us moving, shoes that mean we need an arm to lean on) rather than displaying our individuality and our real selves.

If we could live in a world where the male gaze was eliminated, clothes might be a matter of pure utility and comfort, with a complete rejection of ornamentation. Until that world comes – and it still seems to be some way off – perhaps the best we can do is wear clothes simply because we love them. But how do we test whether we love them for themselves, or because they conform to the male ideal of femininity, which we've absorbed? Tricky, but a good rule of thumb is to be suspicious of clothes that are only for women and to ask ourselves whether a heterosexual man would be prepared to put up with the restrictions or discomfort of that particular garment. Because if something is genuinely good, everyone should want it, right?

So what does feminist dressing look like in the 21st century? It's not trousers instead of a crinoline or dungarees and a buzz cut. It's less about what you wear than what you are comfortable wearing, in body and in mind. I suspect that for many of us, feminist dressing is an attitude rather than an outcome; it's like a comfy, wireless bra rather than a burnt one.

At least for now. It's about trying to find out what we genuinely like to wear and not being afraid to wear those things. It's about accepting ourselves (we'll come back to that later). It's about not competing with other women, it's about lending them our clothes. It's about not wearing clothes that stop us being fully active when we want to be. It's about not wearing clothes that make us feel trussed up or which torture our bodies (with bits of wire in, for instance – wire is for fencing, a poignant reminder of our days as chattels/cattle and not a big feature of menswear). It's about being happy not to wear make-up – even when a man you've just met helpfully tries to remove a mark from your face that is in fact a large freckle. It's about not trying to be anyone else's definition of perfect. Or even our own – the idea of our own perfectibility corrodes and paralyses us.

Above all, it's the awareness, when we look in the mirror, that we might be looking at ourselves with the male gaze, and – if we so much as suspect that we are – making a conscious effort to stick a metaphorical red-hot poker in its eyes. Because a bright flash of defiant, feminist anger in front of the "empty" wardrobe can really help shift that nothing-to-wear feeling.

Dressing for each other

It's often said that women dress for each other. This always feels patronising and it is particularly annoying when the person saying it is a man who, firstly, doesn't realise that as a male he's privileged not to be judged by how he looks and, secondly, is failing to notice the fact that you've bothered to dress up and even put on make-up. Yes, we want it both ways, thanks – having cake and eating it; angry and appreciated – because we're still in a transition period between the long legacy of patriarchy and the kingdom of fairness and equality that is yet to come.

To be fair, it may be that the average testosterone-fuelled male brain can't, rather than won't, pay much attention to clothes. But what is certain is that in purely evolutionary terms, females compete with each other to find a mate and pass on their genes. That is why we don't really like to be wearing an identical outfit to someone else at the party, why designers make sure that two actors don't wear the same dress on the red carpet and why couture houses sell only one of a particular creation per region or country. And yet we are more evolved than that. We value sisterhood, and that includes clothes talk: planning what to wear together, swapping notes on where to buy, getting tips and reassurance. That's why friends and their views on clothes are threaded through these pages.

Getting dressed with a girlfriend can be the best bit of going out – an image flashes across my mind of laughing with my old school-friend Ratty while attaching plastic fish to a net I was wearing before a party with the dress code "surreal" (the event itself is long forgotten). I'm betting you have your own version of that image, possibly not involving a fish. And I know that if I'd had a girlfriend with me when I bought that jumper with ROCK written across the back she would have pointed out to me, as the shop assistant did not, that with my hair falling across it, it looked as if it could say FUCK. She'd have had my back.

We are curious about each other's clothes, and not just in an envious or I-want-that-too way as men may imagine: dressing is not a sports match with a winner. At *Vogue*, if you wore something new, colleagues didn't say you looked good; instead they'd ask: "Who's it by?" – or even: "Whose is it?" (a trap for the uninitiated who might defensively reply: "It's mine!"). And if your new outfit was not "by" a famous designer you still got points for ingenuity. Because this was clothes science, a subject to be studied and learned with the assiduity of a trainspotter, and we do it to varying degrees even if we don't work in fashion. Psychologists have suggested that we are "evolved foragers", with women still shopping like gatherers – considering and assessing whether fruit is ripe, sensitive to texture and smell – while men shop like hunters, with a short burst of focus to get a speedy result. That's certainly the way it goes in my family.

I've noticed, too, that my husband and sons can, almost anywhere, strike up a conversation with a complete stranger about football and, even if the unknown man turns out not to be an Arsenal supporter, they can laugh and josh each other and slap each other's backs. Female football fans can perhaps do the same. But for lots of women, bonding over clothes is the nearest equivalent. And yet it's different from football because it's not an activity; it's about possessions and having stuff. It's about, as John Berger put it, men acting and women appearing. It's about the historical roles of men and women in a patriarchy.

For the same reason, while we obsess about clothes, men tend to obsess about gadgets. They may laugh at our full wardrobes and how long it takes us to get ready and our belief that we don't having anything to wear. And we laugh back at their hoards of tech, most of it now obsolete, their pizza ovens and their car magazines. It is with other women that we feel fully seen and how we look feels most understood – with some notable exceptions (and I confess I'm not married to one).

A woman you don't know stopping you in the street to ask where you bought your coat feels a more profound compliment than "you look nice, is that a new dress?" from a man who's seen that dress many times before. And I suspect it always will.

Two legs good

Of all the pieces of clothing that have restricted women's mobility throughout history, probably the greatest and yet the most overlooked is the skirt. It barely registers because it's so normalised and everyday, and it's so identified with femaleness that, if you want to create a sign to indicate women's changing rooms or toilets, all you need do is fill in the space between the stick man's legs.

The most graphic incarnation of the skirt as impediment is the hobble skirt, which appeared between 1908 and 1912: fashion is always easiest to read when it goes to ridiculous extremes. As the name suggests, hems became so narrow that women could barely walk – a stride might be reined in to a mere two or three inches. Beneath the skirt, to take the strain and stop the seams from ripping, women could wear a "hobble garter" which bound their legs together just like a camel's in the desert. At the same time as the suffragettes were demanding votes for women, some women – in the name of fashion – were literally fettering themselves. Surely not a coincidence.

Skirts not only stop free movement – whether it be the narrowness of the pencil skirt, the bulk of the crinoline or the excess fabric of the floaty variety. Until the 20th century, skirts denied that women had legs and, by extension, the sexual organs towards which legs lead the way. They rendered women as mermaids in the name of modesty – a so-called virtue, which as we've observed, is actually about women being the property of men. So, whether we like it or not, the skirt and the burqa are on the same spectrum.

"I can tell who wears the trousers round here!" is a phrase never used about a man, because men already wear the trousers. They belong to them. It's a phrase used about women challenging male authority. That's how synonymous trousers and male power have become. Little wonder it took women most of history to get our hands on them and our legs inside them.

Skirts and trousers were not always gendered in the West, and in some cultures they are not today. (What is the Sri Lankan lungi or the East African kikoy but a wraparound skirt?) The Romans, who effectively wore skirts in the form of togas and tunics, saw trousers as the symbol of the barbarian, because they were worn by the tribes of northern Europe. These they referred to as *gens bracata*, "trousered people", but eventually the Romans began to wear trousers, too. The soldiers were early adopters, which tells its own story: skirts don't lend themselves to most activities, and evidently these include marching and conquering.

Trousers took various forms. For many centuries, men wore hose (still the word for trousers in German), which were close-fitting, more like the leggings of today.

They allowed the likes of Henry VIII to show off their shapely calves. But the point is, whether they wore hose or breeches or pantaloons, men had cultural permission to reveal their legs as two separate limbs rather than joined together as one.

This difference was upheld by a biblical prohibition against cross-dressing. Deuteronomy 22:5 says: "A woman shall not wear that which pertaineth unto a man, neither shall a man put on a woman's garment; for whosoever doeth these things is an abomination unto the Lord thy God." Admittedly, it's sandwiched between instructions about helping another chap if his ass or ox has fallen down, and not taking both a bird and its mother from the nest, but still, it's there in black and white for the patriarchy to quote if need be. The taboo on women showing that they had legs was so strong that one of the given reasons for burning Joan of Arc at the stake was that she persisted in wearing men's clothes. And later it proved far easier to invent the lopsided contraption that is a side-saddle than to let women wear trousers.

The 19th-century American campaigner for women's rights, Amelia Bloomer, accidentally gave her name (or rather her husband's) to an item of baggy underwear. But it was women's outer garments that she was trying to reform. The idea was to wear trousers like harem pants – wide but gathered at the ankles – beneath a full skirt that fell to just below the knee. This was an alternative to the layers of petticoats that weighed women down. She argued in the 1850s that "the costume of women should be suited to her wants and necessities. It should conduce at once to her health, comfort, and usefulness". Personal adornment was of secondary importance. Bloomer was ridiculed and cartoonists drew pictures of scary women in trousers adopting other manly habits like wearing hats with brims (instead of modest bonnets) and smoking cigars. You don't have to be Freud to deconstruct that last one.

This trousers-under-a-skirt look didn't catch on at the time – it was considered shocking and unfeminine – but it was an early landmark in the first wave of feminism and the dress reform movement. Things sped up in the late 1800s with the invention of the bicycle. Head-to-toe lycra was still a century away, but to be allowed a divided skirt which was less likely to get tangled in the pedals and chain was at least a start. Once middle-class women began to be educated and to play sports there was no turning back, but it was still a long road before trousers were accepted as formal wear. It wasn't until 1969 that a woman wore trousers in the US Congress, and another 35 years before a First Lady – Hillary Clinton – wore them for her official portrait.

Two world wars, when women had to wear trousers to do manual work, made them more socially acceptable: in 1944 sales of women's trousers were five times higher than in the previous year. The sexual revolution of the '60s was another kick in the pants for the male hogging of trousers, but didn't completely change things: girls still had to wear skirts for school just as, for a long time, air stewardesses and City secretaries had to for their work. The 2020 pandemic, when women embraced all-day sweatpants with comfort waistbands, may prove to have been the final nail in the coffin: it felt as if trousers had finally become the default setting for women, too.

It's hard now to imagine a world before sweatpants, so ubiquitous and varied have they become, so at home on the sofa and on the designer catwalk. (They began life in the 1920s when Émile Camuset, founder of Le Coq Sportif, introduced simple, grey, jersey trousers that allowed athletes the freedom to move.) It's harder still to think of an item of clothing that better sums up the changing attitude to femininity during the century since. It is not so long ago that people said: "Pigs sweat, men perspire, but ladies merely glow." Yet today, women blithely wear trousers that are named after a bodily fluid. Whether you call them joggers, track bums or tracky daks (Australia), when you pull on your favourite sweats it's as good a time as any to remember how far we've come. And to enjoy wearing the trousers.

The tale of the handbag

Like trousers, the handbag tells the story of female emancipation. When women's lives were confined to the domestic sphere, there was no need for a handbag because they simply didn't go far enough from home. As ever, the Old Testament was on hand with a cautionary tale about the dangers of women venturing out on their own: when Dinah, only sister of Joseph and 11 other brothers, "went out to see the daughters of the land" and was raped by a man from another tribe, it triggered a shocking, Tarantino-style bloodbath. The book of Genesis doesn't say whether Dinah had a handbag, but I'm guessing not.

Women have always carried food and practical things in baskets or sacks, but the handbag as we think of it today – a private place for personal items and our own money to take out with us in public – is a relatively new phenomenon. In its 250-year history, the handbag has morphed through many incarnations, some of which – the blingy "it" bag, which was only slightly less subtle than tattooing your bank balance on your forehead – are best forgotten. Today lots of handbags are practical and unisex: rucksacks, bum bags or crossbody styles. They leave you hands-free to make a call or send a text, and future generations may wonder what the word "hand" is doing in the word "handbag" at all.

In the Middle Ages, men and women wore a drawstring pouch attached to a cord around the waist – the word "cutpurse" for a thief points out the obvious flaw in this arrangement. When clothes became bulkier in the 17th century, men's garments developed integral pockets, whereas women still wore a "girdle purse" but less accessibly, inside their skirts. That was the beginning of men and women carrying things differently because of how they dressed.

The slimmer silhouette of Empire line dresses in the late 18th and early 19th century (think Jane Austen TV adaptation) was inspired by classical sculpture. Some women even dampened the muslin fabric for more cling factor. This change in outline posed the risk of a VPL (visible pocket line) and so the previously hidden pocket grew handles and was worn outside the clothing once more. Known as a reticule or an *indispensable*, it was at first considered risqué because it was like showing your underwear.

This loss of pockets for women was lamented by Victorian dress reformers. They wanted pockets built into clothes, as they were for men, and viewed the handbag as a symbol of inequality, rather as later feminists would view the bra. But the handbag caught on, bolstered by social changes such as train travel and the advent, in the latter part of the century, of the department store. Women could safely go unaccompanied to these establishments and – critically -- they had toilet facilities. The first public flushing toilets were seen at the Great Exhibition of 1851, and were the beginning of the end for what has been called the "urinary leash" on which women lived (meaning that they could only go as far from home as their bladders allowed). There were, of course, already public toilets for men.

Very gradually, and despite resistance, women were let off the leash and, clutching their handbags, they set out for the department stores. They felt liberated: the ability to go away from home and buy new things was a kind of freedom.

And it can still feel like freedom. Even though we know that consumerism is just another kind of prison.

No pain, no gain

It is one of fashion's supreme ironies that clothes, originally designed to protect us, can cause us harm. There has been a long, dark marriage between fashion and pain. Breathing, for instance, is always useful, but was compromised by the corsets of yesterday just as it is by the so-called "shape wear" of today, which has the same agenda but uses new fabric technology.

Modern tribal markings such as tattoos and body piercings, just like skin scarification in some African societies, are forms of self-mutilation that involve short-term pain for long-term social gain. Other tribal habits (high heels, boned bodices) can bring about life-long skeletal and muscular changes, just like the neck-elongating rings worn by the Kayan women in Myanmar. But these are mere side effects next to elective cosmetic surgery, in which perfectly healthy people end up hospitalised, drugged and cut because they are dissatisfied with themselves. Today "preventive" cosmetic procedures are marketed at young women without a wrinkle to their names.

Consciously or not, we each draw our own line in the sand about how much discomfort we'll endure for how we look. I had my ears pierced (my mother cried), had orthodontic work as an adult, had the odd mole removed and once tried Botox (never again, my head felt clamped in a vice). I wouldn't mind a small tattoo but I could never be sure I'd love it forever so I'll probably remain a blank canvas. That's my line in the sand, and you will have yours.

The French have a phrase for all this: *il faut souffrir pour être belle*. It is necessary to suffer to be beautiful. Because the word "*belle*" (not "*beau*") is used, you can tell that this pearl of wisdom is directed at women, but that should come as no surprise if you've been paying attention. In fact, it is not just necessary to suffer; it is necessary to be *seen* to suffer – to display, as a tribal being, the willingness to belong and to sacrifice oneself to perceived social norms. Thus fashion is not just misogynistic, it has a masochistic element too.

Hans Christian Andersen's famous story of the little mermaid, published in 1837, can be read as an allegory of this. At the age of 15 (puberty), for the sake of a man, the little mermaid takes the form of a woman, with two legs (and, presumably, sexual organs). The price she must pay for entering the human patriarchy is to give up her voice and suffer physical pain: every step she takes feels as if she is walking on knives. Does that scenario ring any bells?

A lot of fashion's pain is focused on the feet. Thanks partly to heel-wearing, which increases pressure on the front of the foot, more women than men end up having foot surgery. But heels, curiously, were first worn by men. They are thought to have come to the West in the early 17th century from Persia (modern-day Iran), where they had long been used by the cavalry to keep their feet secure in the stirrups, just as a cowboy's boots do. Without them there's a risk that the foot slips through the stirrup and the rider is dragged to death.

What started out as a practical, even life-saving, invention soon became a status symbol and, as usual, deliberately impractical. Louis XIV was portrayed in high red heels which, with their military swagger, enhanced his virility – hard as that is to see through modern eyes. They also enhanced his social standing – higher heels equalled higher status – as well as his actual standing: he's thought to have been just five feet four inches tall. He issued an edict that only members of his court could wear red heels, so at once they became a visible sign of royal favour. Charles II spent some of his exile from England at the court of his cousin Louis and picked up this heel habit, bringing it back to England when parliament decided it shouldn't have cut his father's head off after all. Women soon wanted in on the act and became ardent heel-wearers, while by the 1740s men's fashion had sensibly abandoned them.

This gender divide has survived because heels reinforce the roles and rules of patriarchal dressing, rendering the wearer unstable and so more dependent and vulnerable, and flattering by contrast the stability and strength of men (unless they are wearing heels, too). This is depicted in classical ballet, where the female dancers go tortuously en pointe while the male dancers do not. High heels create the optical illusion of slimness and feed unhelpfully into that cultural obsession. They may increase our height, but heels reduce our agency in every other way. My list of things not to do in them includes running, walking on cobbles – particularly in wedges, which create a see-saw effect, and taking public transport (hence the expression "limo shoes", meaning shoes so impossible to walk in that you need a chauffeur). Even though some women have learned to wear them all day long, and indeed certain jobs required them to do so until only recently, for most of us high heels still convey a sense of occasion: for an evening out we literally dress "up". We don't tend to wear heels when we're home alone – a reminder that fashion needs an audience.

The suffering is not just at the time of wearing, although that can be bad enough (top tip: you can get foldable flat shoes to take along in your handbag). Nor is it just the very real risk of a twisted or broken ankle, or other tripping and falling injuries. A list of longer-term damage from heel-wearing reads like the index of a gruesome medical textbook: stress fractures, arthritis, tendinopathy, hammer, mallet and claw toes, plantar fasciitis, knee, hip and back pain. Heels can even affect our digestion. Yet they are unlikely to carry a government health warning any time soon, partly because – unlike smoking – you can't be exposed to passive heel-wearing. That doesn't mean it isn't harmful or making demands on the NHS.

The ancient Chinese practice of foot-binding took the notions of women as both trophy and captive to agonising extremes. To our eyes perhaps the most horrific factor, as with female genital mutilation, is that it was practised by mothers upon their trusting, vulnerable daughters. And yet how many little girls in the West dress up in their mother's high heels, absorbing as they do so their desirability and social acceptance? Even if your mother only wears DMs and trainers, images of women in heels are hard to avoid. We live in a world where you can have Cinderella foot surgery that results in "a narrower, more aesthetically pleasing foot shape" and allows you to "wear certain styles of footwear comfortably" – I think we can guess what those styles are. Just as the skirt and the burqa exist in different places on the same spectrum, so too do foot-binding and high heels.

As the medical side effects of heel-wearing demonstrate, heels affect posture and movement. They make the back arch and shorten the stride to a totter. In particular, as experiments have shown, they exaggerate the sex-specific aspects of female gait, and women walking in heels are perceived by men to be more attractive than those walking in flat shoes. The equation of heels with sexiness is axiomatic, and they've become a staple of pornography.

And yet, despite all this, lots of women say they feel more powerful and assertive in heels, partly because they are nearer eye level with men. A friend who is already on that level (she's six foot tall but describes herself as "five foot twelve") says she longs to wear heels, so strong is their allure. You can, if you want, attend a "strut masterclass" to learn how to walk in high heels and feel empowered, surely a contradiction in terms when it comes to footwear precisely designed to disempower, but there in a nutshell you have the absurd complexity of fashion in all its glory. Even today, in an era of athleisure-dressing and trainer-wearing, the fashion industry can't kick the habit of showing clothes on models wearing heels – especially when they're showing utility and more unisex outfits like boiler suits.

So we ask ourselves, as we stand in front of our wardrobes wondering what to wear on our feet: how much pain for how much gain? Whenever we are tempted to be uncomfortable for appearance's sake – whether it's a pair of teetering heels, a too-tight waistband or the cut of the surgeon's knife – let's remember the little mermaid – the original, which, unlike the Disney cartoon version, doesn't (spoiler alert) have a happy Hollywood ending. With her painful feet and lost voice, she is a good reminder of the age-old pact made by womankind.

And, like any pact, we can break it if we choose.

The C-word

Pull your socks up!... I take my hat off to you... We'll have to tighten our belts.

These phrases all mention items of clothing, but they don't make us reach for our socks, hats or belts. It's the same when we throw down the gauntlet, are slipshod or down-at-heel or putting the boot in, when we are wearing the trousers and waiting to fill dead men's shoes. Clothes are so embedded in our language that most of the time it scarcely even registers. When we decide to revamp something, do we realise we are talking about replacing the top part of a shoe (the vamp)?

Let's invest a moment in seeing how the link between certain words and clothes has become invisible. The word "invest", for a start, which comes from the Latin *investire* meaning "to clothe or cover". In *As You Like It*, Shakespeare uses it that way: "invest me in my motley" means "clothe me as a jester", and it still means "to clothe in the symbols of office" when investing a king or clergy. (Conversely, to take away power is not just divesting but also disrobing or defrocking.) The financial meaning of the word invest came a bit later and conveys the idea of clothing money in a new form. Eventually, it took on its current meaning of committing money in order to earn a return on it.

Similarly, we may not know it, but a "panache" was a plume of feathers on a hat or a helmet, and "bombast" was cotton padding, which is why it means "inflated" or "puffed up". "Shoddy" was a kind of cheap cloth made from shredded bits of old fabric, while "plush" was a soft and luxurious fabric with a long pile.

Still more invisible is the way that words are used to steer us. They can make old ideas seem new; for instance, in the same way that skipping breakfast is now Intermittent Fasting, so baggy clothes are "off-body cuts" and plastic shoes, once inferior to leather, are now virtuously "vegan". Clever use of style names is another ploy: one brand's "Forever Trousers" may help the purchase feel less like an indulgence and more like an investment, while another's "Confidence Blazer", though laughably unsubtle, plants the seed in our minds that it might be just the boost we need. And if "leg-extender trousers" seem to promise a surgical procedure, "broken-in boyfriend jeans" sound good – who wouldn't want a broken-in boyfriend?

Imagine flicking through a fashion magazine or browsing a clothing website that has no words or writing on it. You wouldn't know the brand of the clothes, whether they are this season's or not, new or second hand, the fabric or the price. More importantly, you wouldn't be told what to feel about them – that they are must-haves or on-trend, statement pieces or lovingly created. Nor that they will bring your look right up to the minute, flatter your shape or be an essential part of your capsule wardrobe. We would respond to the objects themselves without the guiding influence of language. Likewise, if you stumbled across the coronation of Charles III on a TV with the sound off and no commentary to explain all the regalia, it would look remarkably like two old people in a church in fancy dress.

Words, which semioticians call "signifiers", point to what is signified, just as clothes themselves do. As Roland Barthes wrote in his 1967 book *The Fashion System*, "it is not the object but the name that creates desire". The visual language of fashion is indivisibly joined to language itself. I have just seen a magazine headline that reads: "The Ultimate Wish List for Now". It makes several assumptions with which it hopes we will not argue: that we want more things, that we want them in such quantity that a list is required, that this particular list is authoritative and definitive and that what we desire now is different from what we desired before. That's a lot of manipulation for six words.

In an age when people queue around the block to see museum exhibitions about designers such as McQueen and Balenciaga, and wealthy people collect handbags as they once collected art and jewellery, it is no coincidence that fashion has appropriated the tropes and language of the art world. High-end designer shops often look just like art galleries, and the atmosphere is equally hushed and reverent. Inside them, the dress is a "piece", of which there may be a "limited edition". And you can be sure the "collection" has been "curated".

Throughout the retail experience, language is used to direct out feelings. It is verbal packaging, the linguistic equivalent of tissue paper and the shop's own carrier bag with ribbon handles, to make shopping feel special and the object precious. It's also verbal dopamine, to keep the mood boosted: Congratulations! You've completed your purchase! Good news! We have dispatched your order!

Just saying.

While we're considering language, it seems only right that we take a quick look at the word "clothes" itself. Like "clothing", it is descended from the Old English *clath*, which in the early Middle Ages could mean "cloth", "clothes", a "covering" or a "sail". Old English was brought by Anglo-Saxon settlers in the fifth century and the word was in fact written *clāþ*. The last letter is called a thorn, which made a "th" sound and which is today obsolete except in Icelandic. (In Middle English, the written thorn gradually changed shape until it looked like a Y and was sometimes mistaken for one: hence we get Ye Olde Tea Shoppe and other pseudo-archaisms that should really begin with "The".) Even further back, *clāþ* came from the Proto-Indo-European *gleyt* meaning "to cling to, cleave, stick", which is after all what clothes do to our bodies, and it is visible in the German word *Kleid* and Dutch *kleed* (meaning "dress"), as well as the Norwegian *klede*, the Swedish *klade* and the Scots *clath* (all of which still mean "cloth").

In the index of the biggest book on fashion that sits on my shelves, there are over 50 entries each under "coats" and "collars", while there are 82 different types of hat (and "see also bonnets, caps"). There are 92 types of shoes listed, and "see also boots" adds another 50. It's a testament to the astounding inventiveness of human beings, their interest in their own appearance and their need for change.

Try saying clothing with a short "o" as in frothing. Or try saying clothes to rhyme with moths (although those are two words you never want to hear in the same sentence). Pronouncing clothes like this reminds us not just of the word's origins but of what we are actually doing when we put on clothes. We are cloth-ing ourselves: wrapping ourselves in cloth.

Label dressing

You know the scene. You are trying on a piece of clothing in a shop, and when you look in the mirror you notice that it hangs better on one side than the other. One seam – usually the one on your left – sits awkwardly, with a little pucker, so that the smooth line of the garment is broken. And you know before you even look: there's a label, or sometimes a whole sheaf of them, sewn into the seam.

When you get home, you might be able to remove the label. Might. It will rarely be clear whether the stitching securing the label is also holding the seam together. But if it is, the whole seam can come undone, and you'll be repairing your new purchase before you've even worn it. Sometimes a helpful dotted line and a pair of scissors is shown, indicating that you should cut the label off. But this, you know from experience, leaves a scratchy little stump, which still spoils the hang. You might be able to pluck out the remains of the label, fibre by fibre, with tweezers, but by now this piece of clothing is starting to feel like a full-time job.

It's the same story with labels at the back of the neck, which can irritate like a mosquito bite and which children often beg to have cut out. These usually display the brand name (significantly, the word label has come to mean brand) and they often have a little, extra-scratchy size tag attached to them – a label on a label.

Why do we need so much writing on our clothes nowadays? The relationship between words and what we wear must, once upon a time, have been so simple. It seems reasonable to assume, for instance, that the loincloth existed before the word "loincloth" did, and that it was centuries, or possibly millennia, before it was necessary to say anything else on the subject. But as soon as clothes began to be described, this relationship became more complex. And once the industrial revolution brought mass production, clothes needed words attached simply to, er, keep tabs on them.

The gap between the signifier and the signified is today a yawning chasm, filled with excess verbiage. Exhibit A is a pair of jeans I bought recently, so bristling with labels they look like the result of a high-speed collision between a wardrobe and a filing cabinet. They came with two cardboard tags on a string plus one stitched through the waistband, all quite easy to remove; inside were five further labels of synthetic fabric, firmly sewn in. Between them they carried more than 700 words, not counting washing symbols, barcodes and numbers. That seems too much information for a pair of trousers.

One of these labels informs me in 31 different languages that "this garment may fade and stain surfaces and/or other garments in lighter colours". So if it does, you have been duly warned. I bought the jeans for the other sort of arse-covering, but I got both kinds. Washing instructions do the same thing: "dry clean only" means the shop can say "I told you so" if you put something in the wash and it comes out ruined or the right size for Barbie.

We need labels to tell us what size to try on, even though sizing is never more than a clue, and we should know where our clothes are made and what they are made from. One label tells me, in several languages again, that my jeans are 98% cotton and 2% elastane. As well as long numbers and a barcode for all their electronic encounters, my jeans have a style name, announced on a tag of its own, presumably to distinguish it from all the other jeans in the shop and to allow internet searchability. All these words and numbers exist because of the sheer scale of the fashion business and the technology that makes it possible.

If I sound grumpy about labels, it's not just because I once had to go to a party with a scratch across my forehead from a tag in a shop. Nor is it because so many labels are just protecting the retailer from liability. Nor even because labels can spoil our clothes. Rather it's because they are physical reminders that the clothes we buy, in which we want to feel individual and to express ourselves, are in fact being churned out on the scale of a natural disaster by the impersonal machine of the clothing industry. The chatter of the labels makes me feel that I'm being processed. Their verbosity makes me nostalgic for a time when clothes didn't have three first names and a surname, and when the country of origin was not a trigger for planetary guilt.

When I stand in front of the wardrobe, as if there wasn't enough going on in there already, my 700-word jeans give me existential angst.

An oblong of cloth

Books on parenting don't warn you that you should expect to find yourself, very late at night, making a costume for the school play out of an old sheet. But that is what happens, and here is what I have learned. The same oblong of cloth, with a slit cut in the middle for the head and a stitch on either side, can multi-task as a Roman citizen (add another oblong tied over one shoulder), any Biblical character (add belt made from a torn-off strip of fabric) and as a medieval peasant (add coloured tights). If it's after midnight, safety pins will do instead of the stitches, but personally I draw the line at staples. All of which is to say that a simple oblong of cloth plays an enduring part in the history of clothing.

We still wear them today, especially in extremes of temperature, and they often form part of traditional dress, whether a sari or a poncho, a Sikh turban or a red-checked Maasai shuka. When humans discovered how to weave, in the Neolithic period, it changed the way we covered ourselves. It's true that the invention of the eyed needle, earlier in the Stone Age, was a critical moment in the dressing of the naked ape. It enabled our ancestors to stitch skins and early materials such as felt, made from compressed or matted fibres, with string, which was fashioned by twisting two fibres together. But it was the invention of spinning and weaving that really got clothes up and running.

This long, slow journey began with the simplest of looms, such as the back-strap loom, where a strap around the body forms one end of the frame, and the ground loom, where the warp threads are tied to poles stuck into the ground. Then for centuries the width of the fabric was determined by the arm span of the weaver, who had to pass the weft thread to and fro from one hand to the other. Wider cloth became possible with the broad loom, which needed two people to pass the shuttle to each other. The invention of the flying shuttle in 1733 was a watershed moment: it meant that a single person could weave a cloth wider than their arm span.

In the modern world, we still turn to simple oblongs of cloth. As soon as the mercury starts to fall, shawls, scarves and pashminas emerge from our wardrobes. But it's in summer – and particularly at the beach – that a rectangle of fabric is virtually all you need. It is a testament to globalisation that we are familiar with so many words for the beach cover-up: sarong is the most used, but there's also the pareo (Tahiti), the kikoy and the kanga (East Africa), and – for men – the dhoti (Indian sub-continent). The lungi, found all over Asia, has the ends sewn together to form a tube, as does the sarong in some countries, such as Sri Lanka.

In the West, sarongs are marketed at women, but

all over the world they are worn by men. They tend to wear them, skirt-style, around the waist – rolled over or tucked or knotted to hold them up – and it's the rest of us who have the creative fun of exploring, in a process that is part sculpture, part origami, the sarong's full versatility. You can make a shorter skirt by folding it in half lengthways before you wrap it around your waist. You can wrap it round you, like a towel after a bath, to form a boob-tube mini-dress. You can hold the corners with the cloth behind you, like a skipping rope at the ready, and cross them over and tie them behind the neck for a halter-neck dress; for a strappier halter you make a single knot at the chest and twist the ends before you tie them.

Once a man selling sarongs on a tropical beach showed me all the different ways he knew of tying them, including a style that he called "breakfast". It's hard to write down the recipe, but the result is a sort of long gilet. He'd realised that these crazy foreigners, who are happy to be near-naked on the beach, like to put something over their swimwear before eating, hence the name. I've since discovered, thanks to a video on Instagram, that by grasping and knotting the two sides at waist level, you can turn the gilet into a dress that is convincing enough to make people ask where you bought it.

An oblong of cloth lies with you in the cradle and the grave, swaddling and shroud. In between it is a versatile raw material, like clay waiting to be formed by our hands. Now that getting dressed has become such a complicated and often fraught business, it is a reminder, in its ancient simplicity, that things don't have to be that way.

The other kind of label dressing

It's no coincidence that the word brand comes from the mark scorched into the hide of a living animal to denote ownership. Commercial branding is a battle for our hearts and minds, and thus our wallets, and the logo needs to be seared into our neural pathways.

Let's remind ourselves what a brand is. The Design Council puts it like this: "A brand is a set of associations that a person (or group of people) makes with a company, product, service, individual or organisation. These associations may be intentional – that is, they may be actively promoted via marketing and corporate identity, for example – or they may be outside the company's control." In other words, a brand is a construct in our collective consciousness.

A Coca-Cola executive once said: "If Coca-Cola were to lose all of its production-related assets in a disaster, the company would survive. By contrast, if all consumers were to have a sudden lapse of memory and forget everything related to Coca-Cola, the company would go out of business." To maintain brand awareness, then, our memories must be constantly jogged. The logo, a symbol or shape that is instantly recognisable, is a shorthand way of doing this. Just as we have deeper feelings for someone we know than we do for a stranger, so too we trust products we feel familiar with.

Our brains change their own wiring after a new experience, and it is this so-called neuroplasticity that branding exploits. When I first saw people with those white wireless headphones sticking out of their ears, I laughed. I thought their wires had fallen out and they didn't realise. I had to learn that it was cool. And then I viewed them in a different way. It's the same thing with platform shoes or flares or huge padded shoulders.

Brands have become increasingly resourceful in the ways they create positive associations inside our heads. They pay for product placement in films and TV series, they gather reflected light from sport by sponsoring events and the players' clothing, they borrow lustre from celebrities by paying them to endorse their wares (high risk these days – one dodgy tweet can bring the whole house of cards crashing down). Brands also enhance their profiles through philanthropy and charitable giving and they run advertising campaigns that are more like mini-movies that hook into our narrative-loving brains. And they disguise branding as entertainment, as in Nikeland – a virtual world that looks like a computer game except that you can do real-life shopping in it.

All of which is fine if you don't mind being covertly brainwashed. The collective imagination of the human species is a wonderful thing – it has, for instance, allowed us to cooperate in large numbers and to become top of the food chain. The downside is that we actually believe in the social reality that we have created: we think we're born with all kinds of things that we actually learn, and as a result, most of our lives take place in a made-up world. Our brains are branding-ready.

The wearer of a brand may think he owns the piece of clothing, but in fact the wearer is "owned" by the brand, in the sense that the ultimate victory belongs to the business. Big brands now search social media for visible logos as a means of identifying potential customers. They've already got value from your post – if the logo is visible, you're helping raise brand awareness, so you're doing their job for them, unpaid – even if the piece of clothing is a fake.

And here's the ultimate conundrum about label dressing, about buying a brand because you want it to be recognised, because you want to signal your success and your tribal belonging. One reason brands are expensive is that, in order to become recognised and desirable, they need to advertise in the right places and and pay rents on shops in the right parts of town and pay PR companies to get their clothes onto the backs of the right people. All that doesn't come cheap, and the cost is passed on to the customer. That means you're not just paying for the clothes you want; you're also paying to be made to want them.

Only you know whether that's how you want to spend your money.

Fire and water

Babies learn by copying, and we don't suddenly stop doing it when we leave the pushchair. Humans are mimetic creatures with brains primed to imitate: it's a key way that survival skills get passed on to the next generation. Even chimpanzees have been observed copying a fashion: one chimp started "wearing" a piece of grass in her ear, and soon others started to do the same. So it is inevitable – with our tribal need to belong – that we copy fashion trends and that they spread like the proverbial wildfire.

There are lots of vested interests that would like to know precisely how ideas spread, not least because if you understood and could control that process, you would have great commercial or ideological power. Memetics, a discipline that dates from the 1980s, uses the model of evolution to explain how cultural information gets transferred. It comes from the word "meme", coined by Richard Dawkins in his 1976 book *The Selfish Gene*, to mean a unit of "cultural inheritance" that carries ideas, practices or behaviours, in the same way that a gene does but without any physical existence. Like a gene, it competes, gets passed on and mutates (just as the word meme has done, come to think of it).

Meanwhile, the epidemiological model suggests that ideas spread as a virus does, by contagion: we get *infected* by fashions. Social media stars and film actors function as super-spreaders. Some academics take this further with the concept that products, behaviours and sneezes are all spread by "networked contagion", and the closer you are to the centre of the network, the more infected – or affected – you will be. Because networks can now be virtual as well as physical, you don't catch ideas like you once caught cholera from living near an infected water pump – geography is largely irrelevant. You are not necessarily more likely to catch a trend if you live in Soho than if you live in the Outer Hebrides.

Or perhaps the whole thing works more like the spread of a religious faith, but speeded up: there is the new idea and its disciples – the so-called early adopters; there are the missionaries of the fashion media spreading the word; and there are the converts, some following enthusiastically, others tagging along because they don't want to be left behind. And then there are the people who are immune, who do not have a clothing-shaped hole in their lives, although it's rare to escape completely unscathed. As one friend once lamented: "I don't pay attention to fashion, but somehow it filters through, and suddenly one day I feel I can't live without a biker jacket." Friends, colleagues, people we pass in the street – they all pass on their influence. You might like something your friend is wearing and ask where they bought it. And if they are a generous, secure and non-competitive friend, they will tell you. In that moment you can see the spark leap from tree to tree. And if they don't tell us? The flames will reach us soon enough.

Another element, water, can also help us understand how fashion works. In the phrase "current fashion", two words that seem to mean the same thing have become inseparable, a tautology we don't even notice. But current means "running, flowing" (from the Old French *corant*, and before that from the Latin *currere*): it is a reminder that fashion is only "now" because it is passing.

Fashion moves tidally, like an ocean; hemlines are a good example. They rose steadily throughout the 20th century, starting at the floor and inching up to the high-thigh in the '60s, before descending to a less revealing point around the knee and back to mid-calf again. Perhaps the slowest ebb and flow in our wardrobes, because it is the most expensive for us to (literally) buy into, is a complete change of silhouette. As the tide of proportion has risen and fallen on the body, the waist has come and gone. It featured above Marie Antoinette's wide pannier skirts but disappeared when the under-the-bust Empire line came along in Regency times. Then it reappeared with the crinolines and, later, the bustles of the Victorians – the extreme "wasp waist" was a kind of spring tide – and by the 1920s had vanished again beneath straight up-and-down flapper dresses which focused on the hip. The reaction to that, the tailored waist of the '40s and '50s, was in turn supplanted by the waist-less tunics and kaftans of the '60s and '70s. And so it will probably go on as long as there's water in the sea.

An unsung benefit of getting older, for those who love clothes, is that you can take a longer view of fashion. What people have worn throughout history becomes as interesting as what you are going to wear tomorrow. Thinking of fashion as an ocean, flowing in currents and moving in tides around the *terra firma* of our bodies, reminds us that – although we can choose to be a fashion victim and get carried far out to sea – we can also just stay on dry land and dip a toe into the water when we feel like it.

The big edit

My friend Pip has a seasonal system for organising her wardrobe: she rotates her clothes with the same rigour as farmers rotate their crops. If you live at a latitude with what are defensively known as "proper seasons", only about half your clothes are needed at any point, so some kind of system seems like a good idea. One spring, when the weather hotted up, I invited myself round to her house to observe this ritual and to take notes. "Come soon," she said, a note of desperation in her voice. "I'm overheating."

The next morning I am in her bedroom as she deftly fillets everything that is warm and woolly, furry or fleecy, from the hangers in her wardrobe and folds them on her bed. Then she gets a large, zip-up storage container from the very top of her wardrobe and extracts from it clothes in cotton and linen, which go onto the empty hangers (trousers on the left, dresses and skirts in the middle, evening wear on the right). She greets them affectionately. There are quite a lot of laundry-intensive white and cream linen trousers. Then the winter clothes are zipped away and manoeuvred onto the top shelf. She is almost apologetic about the hard core of T-shirts, sports kit and underwear that live in the drawers all year round.

I am in awe of my friend's self-discipline and her orderly wardrobe. When I try to analyse why her system works, I realise it's because it's a part of a bigger system that governs the whole way she dresses. She wears a limited, largely neutral palette; darker tones predominate in winter, lighter in summer. Few of her clothes are patterned, and the shapes repeat themselves: tunics, wide trousers, drapey cardigans, '50s-style dresses that go in at the waist. She worked out her personal style early in her life and stuck to it. "I knew what my wedding dress would be like long before I saw it," she says, "and 25 years on I would choose the same one." She doesn't like shopping, so her ears are stopped to the dog-whistle call of the new season, but she would like new versions of what she already has – like replacement parts of a car when they wear out.

So that's what it takes to have a wardrobe like a smooth-running engine: an unwavering sense of your personal style and a heightened immunity to passing trends. Pip never has to encounter an orange-and-pink paisley shirt and wonder what on earth she wore it with. She knows which crops she has planted and is happy to reap them, whereas people like me view our clothes more like a wild-flower meadow, where anything might take root.

Pip always looks good and always looks like herself, whereas I can spend a day feeling uncomfortable because I'm trying out something that doesn't feel quite right. I will hang onto outlandish clothes just in case I might want to wear them one day. I like the freedom to vary what I wear according to the weather or my mood, and to buy something weird and wonderful even if I don't wear it often. For some people, I now realise, their style is a destination at which they have arrived, and for others it is a journey that is never really finished.

Whichever camp you are in, from time to time your wardrobe will need a good clear-out because unfortunately wardrobes obey the basic laws of physics. Until someone invents one that is bigger inside than out like the Tardis, anyone who loves clothes will eventually reach the point where theirs is well and truly full. Exactly when you reach that point depends on a number of variables – volume of wardrobe, rate of shopping, skill at garment folding – but that day will come just as surely as bibliophiles will one day run out of book-shelves. You can buy as many clever storage solutions as you like, but in the end you will have to face up to it: the time has come to chuck out some clothes.

It makes sense to tackle the big edit when spring is in the air because – despite central heating and modern living making the traditional spring clean largely redundant – there is still the vestigial urge to get the nest in order. Even if we haven't got a system like Pip's, the change of season prompts a sartorial shift, so we might as well harness it. People who are not hoarders and are good at letting go of things find the whole process easy: I know one woman who is such a zealous clearer-outer that Monday mornings have seen her trotting down to the Oxfam shop to buy back some item of clothing she's realised she does, after all, require for work. But for those of us who are clingers, who get emotionally involved with our clothes, it's a different story. For us, a riffle through the wardrobe is a vivid trip down memory lane, where a dress can whisk you back through the corridors of time to an important conversation, an amazing party, a compliment received, or a place in the evening sun with the scent of honeysuckle in the air... To throw out such things feels like burning a diary.

Try to catch yourself when you're feeling decisive and upbeat, otherwise the "chuck" pile will still be pathetically small and you'll have to hire a storage unit as your Pending Shelf. Whether you should invite a friend round to help is a moot point: our relationship with our clothes is as intimate as a marriage, and it too can feel a bit crowded with three people in it. How a friend sees you isn't necessarily how you see yourself – you are the authority on that. I'll only get a friend's opinion if I truly cannot decide on my own – for the second round of voting, so to speak.

There's lots of advice out there on tactics. A famous decluttering guru suggests asking yourself certain questions, such as: "Do I have a designated spot for it?" Personally, I think this is letting the tail wag the dog – if we're desperate to keep something we'll find a place for it somehow. She also suggests asking: "Am I showing enough gratitude towards it?" For me that's just ramping up the emotional connection and makes me want to keep that pair of old trousers even more than I did before I felt grateful to them.

There are, however, certain basic questions it can be useful to ask yourself during a clear-out, and I humbly suggest that "is it in fashion?" need not be one of them. Instead, do you love this garment? Do you feel good in it? Do you need it (i.e. for any of the various selves you might present to the world – your work self, your casual self, your glamorous self, your sporting self…)? Does it work (or does it, for instance, ride up or stop you breathing properly)? Do you have other things that do the same job that you like better? Is it high maintenance (this can be anything from being dry-clean only to requiring special underwear)? Would you want to keep it if it had no labels so you didn't know the brand?

It requires a bit of soul-searching, the wardrobe edit. Surely there must be a more scientific way of doing it? Well, if there were a formula, it would ignore the fact that our fantasies and dreams are an important part of ourselves. And it would overlook the fact that women today lead very diverse lives: they might go straight from playroom to boardroom, they might (if they are Pip) be wearing a hat at Ascot one day and competing in a triathlon in a wetsuit the next. They are constantly code-switching. So the clear-out is destined to remain an art rather than a science.

It's fashionable to say that you shouldn't hang onto something if it doesn't bring you joy, but it's asking a lot to expect a favourite old sports bra or a humble T-shirt to bring you joy. Similarly, I've read over and over again that you should never throw out anything that is black, which for me is tantamount to saying: "Keep almost everything, and all the trousers." In truth, other people's rules are only a little bit helpful. It's good to find a positive incentive to let things go: one of mine is having lots of gorgeous nieces and goddaughters who will use my cast-offs much more than I will. But the true key to the big clear-out is knowing and accepting your real self, and the body it is housed in – easier said than done, I know, and we'll dive deeper into that subject later on.

My wardrobe has come a long way. These days, although the hangers are not exactly swishing along the rails, neither are the clothes so tightly packed that getting them out feels like performing a rugby tackle. The living conditions are easier in there now, and I imagine them all stretching their limbs and taking deep breaths. I fancy I can hear a happy sound coming from the wardrobe… it might be my clothes sighing with relief. Or perhaps it is me?

Dress codes

Formal dress codes like "black tie" or "lounge suits" ignore women and speak only to men (I know, who'd have thought?). They seem old-fashioned and irrelevant because they are an echo of a binary age in the multi-gender world we are fortunate enough to inhabit. In an era when any gender can wear anything, when you can put a ball dress with trainers, what is the point of trying to tell people how to dress?

It is true that these days it is hard to get things social-death wrong, and yet the concept of being appropriately dressed lives on. We have developed sensitive antennae for forecasting the social weather so that, when we need to, we can try to get it right. Today, while most dress codes are unwritten, they are still on occasion set down in writing, for avoidance of doubt.

"Occasion" is the key word: invitations to certain formal events, once accepted, involve you in an unspoken contract to play your part, just as much as if you were an actor in a piece of theatre. That includes wearing, more or less, the right costume. You look disdainful of the organiser's efforts if you make none. Parties, like successful plays, need to create an atmosphere, to weave a touch of magic, in order to take flight. They are fragile, airy confections, like spun sugar or candyfloss, which can hold their shape if all the ingredients come together, but can also collapse into a gritty pile. This, more than its original function of social exclusion, is why the dress code still exists.

When a smart invitation arrives, men check their diaries and women check their diaries and their wardrobes. Not necessarily in that order. My husband doesn't think about what he's going to wear until just before a party (and apparently not always then). While for men "black tie" or "lounge suits" give unambiguous instructions, for women they only give the broadest of clues. So we seek them elsewhere, starting with the phone-a-friend call asking: "What are you going to wear?".

Today, to set the key signature for an occasion, invitations might say things like "dress to party", "summer smart" or "dress up", as well as the familiar, oxymoronic "smart casual". None of them is specific, nor do they give a clear steer even for men (fancy dress also levels the playing field). But when decoded, they all mean the same thing: "Be comfortable. No need to go over the top. But please make an effort, because we have."

Men can thank Charles II and Beau Brummell for making their lives simpler when it comes to clothes – or blame them for making them boring, depending on their viewpoint. As well as importing the trend for high heels, Charles brought back from his stretch of exile at the French court the embryonic jacket-and-waistcoat combination – mentioned by Pepys in his diary – that would grow up to become the three-piece suit. It was then a close-fitting, sleeved vest reaching to the knees, worn with a longer, narrow-sleeved coat. This was the beginning of the end for the peacock phase of men's fashion in Europe, when aristocrats had adorned themselves as extravagantly and colourfully as possible.

In the 1790s, George Bryan (aka "Beau") became friends with the Prince Regent, later George IV, and famous for his personal style, which was hugely influential. His bold simplicity of dress was adapted from the sporting wear of the English country gentleman, with military touches – a studiously pared-down but finely tailored look. For evening, he favoured a blue or black tailcoat, white waistcoat, black pantaloons or knee breeches, white cravat and thin shoes called pumps. This elegant but restrained way of dressing was soon required at London's most fashionable clubs, and evolved into the Regency wardrobe familiar to us from screen versions of Jane Austen novels. Brummell's style established the basic garments and the monochrome palette that live on in today's suits and dinner jackets.

Perhaps the tide will turn, but for now it is women who bear the uncertainty about what to wear on formal occasions, and who give up headspace to getting it right and diary space to shopping. Formal wear for us can mean anything from trousers to a ball gown so, like the rest of the sisterhood, I carry on fine-tuning my antennae for clues. The venue and the reason for the occasion (wedding? awards ceremony? barmitzvah?) give hints, as does the invitation itself (email? thick card?). But the really big question – bigger than short or long, trousers or skirt – concerns footwear, specifically heels. Better than vague, two-word clues like "casual chic" would be an estimate of the amount of time to be spent standing up versus sitting down: "mostly seated", for instance, or "standing for drinks then perching slightly uncomfortably while you eat a buffet dinner". It would be ideal, too, to know about the music, so that we can work out whether we'll want to dance the night away.

Imagine my joy when one summer a big, black-tie anniversary dinner was preceded by an email with the subject line "Flats or heels?". "You will need," it read, "to negotiate cobbles, wide stone steps, gravel, decking and grass if you choose to go outside the marquee. The flooring in the marquee is carpeted and firm under foot." I hardly need say that it was written and sent by a woman. Never mind putting dress codes on the invitation; as long as women persist in wearing heels, a guide to the going, as at a racecourse, is far more useful.

Mutton

Even the dog can tell by my footwear whether we are going for a walk. If I wore ballet slippers or high heels, she would register surprise (but she'd still come for a walk). Humans have the same skill, honed over years of observation just like the dog's, but way more refined. We know what looks "right" and feels appropriate with an accuracy that feels like an instinct when it is really – to borrow Napoleon's words about history – "but a fable agreed upon".

There are social constructs galore about women "dressing their age". Here's an actual headline from *The Times* newspaper: "Should you wear ripped jeans over 40?" It's clear from the picture of a glamorous woman with long, grey hair that 40 refers to years rather than, say, degrees centigrade or metres above sea level. And even without the picture we'd have known what it meant, because – despite the anti-ageism movement – we live with the residue of centuries of prejudice about what older women should wear. And until very recently, the menu choice has been mutton dressed as lamb, or just plain mutton.

We say that of course everyone should be free to wear whatever they want at any age. But with the next breath we catch ourselves lamenting our bingo wings and wondering whether we can still wear a bikini or a sleeveless top. We are so steeped in the culture that judges us as we age that we do it ourselves. I was horrified when my mother had her gloriously thick, long, chestnut hair cropped short when she turned 40 because she "didn't want someone behind her to get a shock" when she turned round. She is an extreme case, I admit. She is also a product of her time, and today there is more permission for women to age as they please and appear as they want to rather than becoming shapeless, sexless and invisible forms. But, as Hollywood's persistence in casting young women opposite old men demonstrates, it is still very much a work in progress.

Attitudes to women ageing might seem at first glance to be underpinned by biology, because women who are past child-bearing age are not directly useful to the survival of the species. When it comes to mate selection, therefore, mutton dressing as lamb is a kind of false advertising. This is a proprietorial, male-gaze perspective on the role of women, of course, and the fable agreed upon is that beauty is youth, youth beauty. Underpinning this is a US$100 billion worldwide cosmetics market that helps create the illusion of child-like plump lips, large eyes and smooth skin on our ever-ageing faces.

We live in a youth-obsessed culture that treats ageing like a disease to be cured, a "semi-death", as Simone de Beauvoir put it. A lot of the societal fear of death is projected onto women as they age, perhaps because their wombs once literally embodied life itself. The received wisdom that older women shouldn't wear black because it is "draining" to the complexion has more in my view to do with its association with death and mourning in our culture: it turns us into uncomfortable *memento mori*. It also conjures up witches and widows: black-clad women whose very existence challenges the precepts of the patriarchal order.

On a good day, ageing feels like a relief: it's the opposite of being a self-absorbed teenager trying to be cool and thinking that everyone is watching you. You can do, be and look as you want, and if anyone chooses to judge you that's their problem. On a bad day, when the rollercoaster of the menopause flings your body around and you barely recognise yourself, it can trigger feelings of loss and self-doubt, which get channelled into a new, midlife wardrobe anxiety. On days like these, I can recommend leaning in, defiantly wearing as much black as possible and seeing yourself as not mutton, nor lamb, but a fierce she-wolf in sheep's clothing.

When beauty no longer comes "free with the hormones", as Ursula Le Guin expressed it, there is a gradual change in how we spend our appearance-related hours. Briefly, it involves less shopping and more maintenance. Fewer new looks, because you've worked out what you like, and more comfort, because you start to have odd aches and pains, so why take any extra grief from your clothes? High heels stop looking glamorous and start looking dangerous. As you age, just like a car, you spend more time in the garage, and you notice it's the engine and the fuel that keep you on the road, not the groovy respray and the go-faster stripes.

You realise what the fashion industry would prefer you not to realise until you've got decades of spending under your designer belt: that the true investments are not a new winter coat or this season's flared trousers, but rather your health and your fitness. And your teeth. The clothes you were once so thrilled with are long gone, but your body is still here, keeping on keeping on, if you're lucky. Do treatments like Botox and fillers qualify as one of these investments? Probably not. They're more like the groovy respray. They do not prevent ageing; they just present a different, distorted version of it. In the interests of avoiding needles in the face, perhaps it helps to reframe how we see ageing skin, to think of it as a different and interesting new fabric instead of an old one that has been spoilt by too many washes.

Crepe is not the same as silk, but it is still a beautiful material.

Sequins in the desert

Nail varnish and sand do not go together like a horse and carriage, which is one of life's little ironies for people like me who only bother to paint their toenails when heading for the beach. Sand is a brilliant exfoliant for the feet and it doesn't spare your pedicure. One summer, on a coarse-sand beach, I gave up on grooming and went bare-toed. I soon had beach hair, too – salty and stiffly textured. Call it what you like – laziness, letting myself go or simply relaxing – before long I was a shine-free zone. And I realised that our natural state is to be matt not glossy.

Throughout history, shiny things have been synonymous with progress and power – the computer screen I'm in front of now is a recent example. In the Bronze Age, the gleam of metal signified success just as, in the Gold Rush, the glint in the panhandler's sieve meant the hope of it. The bright glow of treasure illuminated the dark world in which *Beowulf* was written and, in the dim light of an early Greek Orthodox church, the magic of an icon resided in the gleam of its gold paint.

Modern cities are shiny, slick things, covered in metal and glass. Patent leather looks fine on Bond Street but weird on a beach, just as sequins look fine in a night-club but trashy at the seaside, like tinsel in summer. It's not a coincidence that glamorous fabrics – silk, satin, velvet – have a sheen to them that signals sophistication and urbanity. We dress "up" in them – the equivalent of a skyscraper clad in gleaming glass – while we dress "down" in textured tweed or dull denim when we encounter the wide horizons of the countryside or the sea.

The dustiest place I have ever been is the road in Tanzania that goes past the Olduvai Gorge – the jeeps travelling along it send up thick plumes of dust, covering themselves in it as if they were part of the landscape and the earth was trying to reclaim them. Olduvai is where Louis Leakey's excavations proved to the world that Africa was the cradle of humankind, our place of origin. Our creation myth tells the same dust-to-dust story: we were made from the earth and we go back to it.

People are not shiny, despite the REM song. We are uncut diamonds. Our shine is on the inside – when cut, like a diamond, we glisten – and in our bodily fluids (blood, sweat, tears, spit, semen). We are containers of liquid, glimpsed in our open eyes and mouths, and some of that liquid is our life blood. Without it we return to dust. Is our magpie-like attraction to shiny stuff, then, part of our quest for immortality?

The human body can last for weeks without food but only a few days without water, so our brains are conditioned to spot the gleam of water from afar: in the dust-scape of our beginnings it was a matter of life and death. Experiments have shown that thirsty people have a preference for glossy paper, and that even four-year-olds prefer images with a glossy rather than a matt finish. We are drawn to the thing that helped our ancestors survive. It shows up in our jewellery boxes and our wardrobes. And at the beach, like sequins in the desert, on my toenails.

On reflection

We're not really designed to see ourselves. It is very difficult to see your own reflection in a puddle – what you mostly get is a silhouette of yourself against the sky.

For millennia before the first mirrors were made, such an imperfect glimpse of him- or herself was all that was available to *Homo sapiens*. Portraits were only for the rich, and anyway they did not show you live and moving. They froze a moment in time, which meant that in Ancient Rome sculptures were sometimes made in two pieces so that the hair could be updated later. Similarly, in the 18th century, Gainsborough had to be recalled over a decade after painting the Linley sisters to bring their hair-look right up to date.

Can you imagine not knowing how you look? Today, we are not only surrounded by mirrors themselves, which are everywhere from the bathroom to the gym to the lift at work, but also by all those incidentally reflective surfaces such as cars, computer screens and the oven door. It is hard to avoid your own reflection, even if you want to. With the advent of the selfie and social media, our curated view of ourselves has become social currency. Surely we are approaching peak self-regard?

The business of looking at ourselves is, um, reflected in our language. We know that it is not a compliment to say that someone is self-regarding, and if you are asked how you see yourself, you don't reply "by looking in a mirror". That's how fused the literal and metaphorical aspects of seeing have become. It's worth uncoupling them a bit if we want to remain sane in a culture that exhorts us to change what we see in the mirror – by buying this object or having that procedure – in order to feel better. How we appear and how we feel are not the same thing, but they have become enmeshed, ably assisted by the mirror.

The earliest mirrors, found in Anatolia, date from around 6,000 BC and were made of polished stone. From about 2,000 BC, there were mirrors of polished copper in Ancient Egypt and of bronze in China. These surfaces would have shown a much dimmer reflection than we are used to today.

The Romans knew about glass backed with metal, but the privileged few who owned mirrors still saw themselves through a glass darkly. With high-definition hindsight, that might have been a blessing.

It was not until the early Renaissance that mirrors made with a tin-mercury amalgam became more common in Europe. Even then, they remained one of the most expensive possessions a person could have, and the Church disapproved because they led to the dangerous path of self-worship (turns out it had a point). Only when the secret of mirror making was stolen from the island of Murano, thanks to a spot of industrial espionage on behalf of Louis XIV, did mirrors become more affordable. He built the Hall of Mirrors at Versailles, with 357 mirrors shiny as a guillotine's blade…

It was a German chemist who, in 1835, invented the silvered-glass mirror that ushered in the world as we know it, with mirrors, mirrors everywhere. Today there are shops with mirrors in the fitting rooms that can take payment right then and there – you hold the barcode to its gleaming surface, followed by your payment card. You can then walk straight out of the shop without queueing at the till – and with no time to change your mind.

Mirrors have great benefits – solar power, precision telescopes, spinach-free teeth – but what is it doing to us, meeting our own reflection at every turn? Before the looking glass, others saw us far more than we saw ourselves: for most of history, humans were probably only seen by a few hundred people in their lifetimes, until they started to live in cities, when perhaps that number increased to a few thousand. Without a mirror, you could only see part of your body and nothing of your face, and you looked out at the world from within: it was an inside-out process. Now that is largely reversed: an outside-in process in which our interior selves are bombarded with information about our exteriors – along with suggested improvements. The mirror has made us subject and object at the same time.

Often there's a mirror on the inside of the wardrobe door. It spends most of its life shut in the dark with your clothes, lying in wait. But when it sees the light – when you are getting dressed – there it is, ready to reflect your own doubts and fears right back at you.

Our native land

Imagine you are standing next to a stranger and you are both looking into a large mirror in front of you. You do not both see the same thing. They get an overall impression of you, and you of them, while each of you will apply a different level of scrutiny to your own image – more detailed, more assessing. Your eye will probably be drawn to the bits of you that you feel insecure about, wondering if you look OK, checking your hair and possibly wishing you hadn't had that almond croissant for breakfast. This is body image – the thoughts and feelings we have about our physical selves. We can only know someone else's body in the way that we know a foreign country, but our own body is our native land. And we don't always love the country we live in.

Precisely how much we don't love it is becoming alarmingly clear. Four-fifths of people aged 12 to 21 say they dislike their bodies and are embarrassed by the way they look. Body dissatisfaction makes you more vulnerable to eating disorders, for which hospital admissions increased by 84% in the five years to 2021. Although the number of young men admitted more than doubled in that time, a large majority of those affected are still young women.

Body image has a complex and widespread root system. The deep tap root is the way that the patriarchy, with the help of religion, uses social shame to affect how women view their bodies. Nearer the surface are side roots such as the current ideal body shape, which we internalise, and family environment, a micro-culture in which body image – positive or negative – is passed from parent to child. Another entrenched part of the root system is the transformational myth – if we change this or buy that, life will improve. As if by magic.

If you tried to invent a mechanism that increased body dissatisfaction, you couldn't come up with anything more effective than social media, with your friends' filter-on versions of themselves and celebrities' retouched images pinging into your pocket. Plastic surgeons talk of "Snapchat dysmorphia", and one reports an increased demand for nose jobs from young women who don't realise that a selfie taken at arm's length is as distorting as a fairground mirror. (He doesn't mention that cosmetic surgery is itself a distortion.) Inside our heads, the fictive body lives alongside our actual body.

Entwined with all of these roots are business interests. In order to survive, many industries need us to obsess about our bodies – not just the cosmetic surgery industry (the global market worth of which was over US\$63 billion in 2021), but also the diet or "weight management" industry (US\$142 billion) and the clothing and fashion industry (which generated US\$2 trillion per annum before the pandemic hit). For their financial health, these industries need to play on our insecurities about our physical selves: not so healthy for us, then.

Because of these "merchants of body hatred", as Susie Orbach calls them, commercial pressures have entered into our experience of ourselves. They are hard to outwit: a few years ago, a Californian woman invented a "skinny mirror", which made you look a dress size smaller – a self-deceit, yes, but worth a try when our weapons against body fascism are so limited. But before long, retailers began to buy the mirror for their fitting rooms to get people to buy more clothes… and sure enough, sales went up. There could hardly be a more graphic illustration of the way that business has hijacked our view of ourselves. And perhaps the brutal truth is that the price we pay for free-market capitalism is a percentage of the population with body dysmorphia – the casualties of an economic system.

Accepting our bodies – or better still forgetting about them – is a formidable task when there are so many vested interests pestering us. In reality, most of what makes us ourselves is not (as Michael Jackson so helpfully demonstrated) subject to successful alteration: our height and build and colouring are our life companions. Unless you are obese, the changes made by diet and exercise are at the margins – you still look like you, more or less toned, perhaps, a bit curvier or a bit leaner, but basically you.

Until we accept our bodies naked, we are unlikely to

be satisfied with the clothes we put on them. But if we could acknowledge who we are, whether we're a Rubens or a Giacometti or somewhere in between, we might finally see that getting dressed is 99% about acceptance and only 1% about shopping.

The reminiscence bump

We are born naked, but soon we are wrapped in a piece of cloth. Then, for years. someone else puts clothes on us, and we are helped to dress until we develop the fine motor skills required to tie laces and do up buttons. But even when we've mastered the mechanics, it is not until adolescence, when we start to separate from our parents or carers, that we begin to dress ourselves in the fullest sense of the word: seeking to express our identity, our independence and our tribal allegiances through what we actively choose to wear. Experimenting with what we wear, learning to put it all together in our own way and buying it with our own money... all of this is not just an extended metaphor for growing up but a critical part of it.

It is not always a smooth handover – there may be a breakaway tussle or total war over a particular piece of clothing. Mine, boringly, was not about a safety pin though the nose but heels that my mother deemed too high. Still, whether it's a too-short skirt or an extra piercing or three, a full red Mohican or just an ugly pair of trainers, appearance is an easy way to articulate teenage rebellion, not least because it saves the effort of an actual conversation while being as clear as a V-sign. Which is particularly handy when the brain is undergoing an epic remodelling project, as it does in puberty.

One aspect of this is that the connections between the emotional and decision-making parts of the brain are still developing. But something else is happening in the brain at this point, too: it is laying down lasting memories. One of the most robust findings in the field of memory research is the phenomenon known as the "reminiscence bump": the fact that we remember more from our late adolescence and early adulthood than we do from any other part of our lives. Since this bump was first observed in the 1980s, various theories have been put forward to explain it: that our late teens and early twenties are a period of rapid cognitive change when the brain is learning and storing what it will need; that there may be an age-related coding efficiency that causes more memories to be stored at this time of life; that this is a time of identity formation and self-creation, when we define and refine who we are; and last but not least, that we are doing so many things for the first time and our brain likes novelty, as we've already seen. The reminiscence bump is possibly a cocktail of all of these factors.

The reminiscence bump coincides with the rapid hormonal changes and consequent physical growth in our bodies. And it is the time when not only are we shaping our identities and learning to dress ourselves, but also, crucially, our core body image is being formed. It follows that teenagers with mental health issues

– mostly girls, who thanks to social media, can now be exposed to the objectification of women 24/7 – are likely to carry intense memories of this period into their future lives. Hence my skinny friend who was fat as a teenager and still thinks of herself that way.

Is there anyone who can't recall a cruel comment made to their teenage self? Later in life, if we have a moment of uncertainty as we get dressed – one of those sartorial identity crises that can suddenly overwhelm us – we may be able, if we pay attention, to scent the brimstone whiff of teenage angst. Because our formative years were the ones when we really did have nothing to wear – nothing, at any rate, that could contain our developing bodies and express our emergent sense of self. The years when our identities were still a work in progress.

The House of Worth

It is a happy accident of history that the man credited with revolutionising the business side of fashion was born with the surname Worth. Charles Frederick Worth was an Englishman who went to Paris, and in 1858 founded one of the first and foremost fashion houses. He has a lot to answer for because, to promote his clothes, he started sewing his brand label into them and using live models instead of dummies. And look where all that ended up.

These promotional tactics were a great success and the House of Worth dressed the Empress Eugenie, the famous actresses Lily Langtry and Sarah Bernhardt and endless European society women, as well as a steady stream of American heiresses who sailed across the Atlantic in part to stock their wardrobes with the latest trends. One such was Edith Wharton, who, perhaps as a pun, titled her 1905 novel, about a woman who is edged out of New York's high society because she fails to make a suitable marriage, *The House of Mirth*.

Worth's Anglophone clients must have found his

name quietly reassuring. In fact, it hides in plain sight one of the slipperiest issues in the field of fashion: how we determine value, both financial and non-financial. The former is relatively easy: an object is worth what someone will pay for it. In 2020, Sotheby's New York sold an Hermès Ombre Lizard Birkin bag for US$137,000, which is doubtless a great deal more than it cost to make (unless you're one of the lizards). There are more expensive Hermès bags, but I think that just sticking on diamonds is somehow cheating.

Worth in its non-financial sense, of being useful or important or good, is harder to define. I once read a short story about a blind man who marries a woman with a large birthmark on her face, which he doesn't know about because he can't see. They are blissfully happy until one day he overhears some people commenting on his wife's disfigured face... and this knowledge curdles his love for her, spoiling the marriage. I mention this tale because it so brilliantly illustrates how what we value is affected by what is valued by the world around us.

Worth is socially endorsed: it is the invisible equivalent of body image. In a consumerist culture, where endorsement is loud and persistent and we are constantly being told what to want, it can be hard to stay in touch with what actually matters to us individually. That is why "because you're worth it" is one of the cleverest as well as the most insidious slogans ever invented in the world of advertising. It uses what ad folk call a "social enrichment" message: that is to say, it doesn't just tell you what the product does, but how it will make you feel.

Born in the early 1970s in the first person – "because I'm worth it" – the slogan co-opted the language of feminism to sell hair dye to women. (It worked.) Sure, it was an improvement on the male-voiceover and man's-viewpoint ads that had gone before, but it still operated in the murky waters where appearance, self-esteem and shopping dissolve into each other. It mixed up different kinds of worth.

Over time, the phrase morphed into "because you're worth it", a shift to the second person which, deliberately or not, speaks of the social-validation aspect of worth: it's someone else telling you you're worth it. Today, in the name of inclusivity, it has become "because we're worth it". And, coincidentally, we're worth a lot to L'Oréal's balance sheet, too.

One conundrum of being a social animal is how to strike a balance between the private and the public self, what we feel about ourselves and the messages we receive about ourselves from others. It's no simple matter because the two are connected like the sides of a Möbius strip. We do need a certain degree of social approval, yes, but not from 5,000 of our closest friends liking a selfie taken while we wear false eyelashes and pouty lips.

How to build a genuine sense of self-worth and inner confidence, while growing up exposed to the superficial, appearance- and possessions-based values of social media and reality TV, is far from obvious. It is particularly hard for young women, who are told that they are equal to men but can see they are treated differently – objectified, sexualised and judged by how they look; who see that women still bear most of the domestic burden; who know that what they choose to wear may one day take the blame for male violence. The uptick in self-harming and mental health disorders suggests that the virtual world does not offer a nourishing diet. Let's not reserve judgement until we have more data, as scientists must do: let's trust our guts on this one.

Whatever the advertisers and retailers would have us believe, we cannot dress our way to self-confidence, or shop our way to self-love.

Being worth it is not the same as knowing your worth.

Naked truth

I've spent a substantial chunk of my life in rooms where everyone is wearing clothes except for one person. It doesn't feel awkward or exploitative: there is an atmosphere of trust and respect, and the air is heavy with concentration, silent with the sound of total absorption, except for the occasional squeak of charcoal on paper.

Life drawing is an artistic discipline that grew out of the Renaissance infatuation with depicting the human body and was formalised in the academies set up in the 17th century. Students drew first from prints and plaster casts before they were allowed to progress to drawing from live models – hence the name. Life drawing has been a core element of traditional art training in the Western world ever since, and has figured in my life since I was 16.

It is more testing to draw the human body than a still life. A vase looks plausibly like a vase even if the proportions are wrong, but when the angle of a shoulder or a hip looks impossible we instinctively know it. We know so much about bodies from inhabiting them and from living with each other: we are intimately acquainted with the way our flesh is a clothing for our bones.

Not everyone understands the appeal of hours spent staring at a naked stranger, making marks on a piece of paper with pencil, graphite, pastel, crayon, charcoal, ink, paint, or any combination of the above. But for me it is an utterly absorbing process, an escape from daily routine, a forgetting of troubles, a moment of suspended animation. The still point of the turning world. I feel humbled that the models are willing to undress so that students like me can look and learn, and it never occurs to me to judge or evaluate their bodies. I accept them in all their individual complexity and idiosyncratic glory. The more they sag and bulge and wrinkle and hang and droop, the more interesting they are to draw. Words like ugly or beautiful, fat or slim, have no meaning here; they are like words from another planet where a different language is spoken. Life drawing is an experience that feels almost sacred in its acceptance of how things are.

Why, then, is it so hard to transfer that same sense of peace to my own body? You might think that, if you spend a lot of time looking at naked people of all shapes and sizes who are comfortable taking their clothes off in front of strangers, you would become more accepting of all bodies, including your own. It ain't necessarily so.

We are our own harshest critics. We tend to judge ourselves far more unkindly than we do others. And so we try to redraw ourselves.

The courtroom in the head

If your best friend keeps asking you: "Are you OK? Are you sure you're OK?" and then, after a short pause: "There's something wrong, isn't there?", in the end you start to wonder. Perhaps you're not really OK? Perhaps the friend has noticed something you haven't? You begin to doubt yourself.

This, in essence, is what our brain does to us. It's constantly checking we're safe, how we're doing, whether there are any threats around. It does so with the best of intentions, to keep us safe and sound, and to prime us for action if need be. Remember the brown shape behind the bush? It could be a rock or it could be a lion, but we must always assume it's a lion. It is possible that extremely chilled cave men and women did exist, but they would not have been the ones who survived. Theirs are not the genes that got passed down to us. Contentment is a potentially life-threatening state, so we are condemned to be ever alert and inquisitive.

On the plus side, this means that thinking and planning are our superpowers: our curious, questioning brains have allowed us to construct elaborate civilisations and work out how to fly and build bridges and weave wide fabric and live longer. They are extremely good at problem solving. On the minus side, they also ask us questions about ourselves: not just whether we are safe, but our position in the primate group – where we sit in the dominant hierarchy – with all the implicit comparison of ourselves to others that that brings. And they are hard to switch off: as a species we are compulsive thinkers, worrying about the future, regretting the past, always seeking ways of making improvements rather than enjoying the moment. This is what lies beneath the self-assessing voice in our head asking: how do I look? how am I doing? do people like me? Would it be better if I did this or said that, if I looked different or wore something else? If my nose was smaller or my dress was new? If I was taller or slimmer…? This process of continuous self-judging has been called the courtroom in the head: it's a brilliant description, except that this courtroom never seems to adjourn for lunch.

As well as keeping up this nagging, critical self-talk, our brains display "negativity bias", the cognitive trait that means we remember and pay more attention to unpleasant experiences and events than we do to pleasant ones. News coverage reflects this – bad news grabs our attention, however much we say we long for good news – and experiments have shown that we learn faster from negative experiences than from positive ones.

Most of us have felt this: a negative comment about us hooks into our heads like Velcro, while positive ones seem to slide off as if they've landed on Teflon. When we see a photo of ourselves, our eye goes to the bits we don't like. All of this is confirmation, if we needed it, that the brain is an organ of survival and that happiness is not relevant for the continuation of the species. So we should not be totally surprised that we are our own harshest critics. Or our own worst enemies – the fact that we have two phrases for attacking ourselves tells its own story.

When famine or predators could be lurking around every corner, our atavistic alertness to novelty and danger was crucial. In the modern world, where our basic needs of food and shelter are met, it is less so. In fact, it can become a positive disadvantage in an always-on world with so many new things and distractions, where we are always checking our phones and returning messages. This constant multi-tasking – which should more accurately be called task-switching – carries a significant cost to the brain, increasing as it does the production of the stress hormone cortisol as well as the fight-or-flight hormone adrenaline. It also creates a dopamine-addiction feedback loop which rewards the brain for losing focus and seeking yet more stimulation, so that it becomes increasingly hard to concentrate.

These are not the optimum conditions for the court-room in the head to function in a balanced way. Thriving on the fact that our overstimulated brains don't have time to stop and think, fuelled by the compare-and-despair culture of social media, our fault-finding inner critics have a field day. They tear into us, questioning ourselves, our bodies, what we wear and the very purpose of our existence.

In today's courtroom in the head, the defence barrister has gone AWOL with exhaustion and the judge is biased against us. There's almost no chance of a fair trial. Instead, we end up sentenced to a life of body dysmorphia, depression and shopping, with little chance of parole.

Don't just buy something!

If the unquiet mind is the price we pay for evolutionary success and if we can't silence our inner critic, then we can at least get to know it. We can try to learn more about the proceedings of the courtroom in the head. If we succeed in doing that, we are less likely to be ambushed by self-doubt and suddenly find ourselves in possession of a new dress we really don't need. In other words, we need to know our own mechanisms.

How do we get to know the habits of our own mind? If we try to empty it, to make it concentrate on one simple thing – the breath, for instance – we quickly notice how it wanders. It does what the mind has evolved to do, exploring and bouncing around from one thing to another like a curious puppy. As soon as we label this activity "meditation", the inner critic pops up to wonder whether we're doing it right and whether we'll ever be as good at it as the Dalai Lama. But we also start to observe where the mind wanders to, and that is an instructive thing to know.

I mention the word "mindfulness" with trepidation,

because in the age of mindful cooking and mindful art galleries it has become distorted and devalued. But Mindfulness Based Cognitive Therapy (MBCT), which combines ancient wisdom with modern psychological science, is underpinned by robust scientific evidence. It is recognised by the NHS and, while it was first developed to treat depression, it has been retooled to help improve mental health and wellbeing for anyone who is interested.

A few years ago, I did a short MBCT course and found that its focus on being rather than doing, of paying non-judgemental attention in the present moment and of accepting things as they are, was a valuable respite from the cultural noise and overstimulation of 21st-century life. I won't try to summarise the whole course, but suffice to say that by the end of it I felt able to observe the cogs turning in my mind from a distance rather than being completely caught up in them.

Despite the tireless efforts of my inner critic, I gradually became much more aware of where my mind wandered off to. And I was shocked to discover how often it headed straight for the wardrobe and had a good rummage around inside. I saw my mind wondering what to pack for the weekend or wear to a party, whether to throw out that army jacket or shorten those trousers, whether I looked good in this outfit or ugly in that one. I realised that thinking about clothes was taking up quite a lot of headspace. And I resented the time it wasted.

It is useful to catch ourselves in these moments of

anxious self-evaluation: they show us what our issues are. In particular, they show us what we rely on to feel good about ourselves. For me and for others, for numerous reasons that we've already examined, it often concerns appearance and whether we look "right". With these feelings front and centre, it is easy for the mind to get hooked on what we wear, own and consume.

Meditative practice, which aims to develop attitudes of acceptance and non-striving, can act as a counterbalance to this. It can teach us that paying attention is a choice, which is something of a life skill in a free-market economy where our attention is commoditised. Yet it can be difficult to interrupt what you're busy with, sit down and try to meditate: your brain doesn't want to unhook from all that addictive phone-checking and constant doing. And that very difficulty is itself the measure of how much it is needed.

One of the useful phrases I picked up on the course is "don't just do something, sit there!". I may not have become the world's best meditator – sometimes I forget about it for months – but I'm more aware of how my own mind behaves and tries to get me to comfort-consume, and more able to choose where I place my attention. It's as if the rickety gate on some neural pathway is now propped open. At least some of the time...

If we can manage to keep the gate to self-awareness open, we can sometimes adjourn the courtroom for long enough to recognise our inner critic as the voice of our fears. Even if we just do this for a moment – taking

time out to pause and breathe, to ground ourselves –
we can take a step towards accepting ourselves and our
bodies as we are.

The constant striving of fashion, which feeds on the
dissatisfaction caused by the restless mind, is the very
opposite of acceptance. But with practice and more
awareness, we can start to block our ears to the siren call
of consumerism. The mindful wardrobe accepts itself
as it is.

So: don't just buy something, sit there!

Resistance tactics

Mindful awareness is probably our strongest weapon against the dark forces of consumerism, but there is other ammunition at our disposal. Here are some resistance tactics that I hope might work for you when the wardrobe seems empty and the urge to splurge descends:

Go monochrome: turn your phone screen to its black-and-white setting. Most clothes look considerably less alluring when the colour is drained out of them. Research also shows that colour makes images more memorable.

Be grateful: the 10-finger gratitude practice is a mindfulness exercise in which you hold each finger in turn as you find 10 different things to appreciate in your life. Some of these could of course be clothes that have served you well. It's a useful counter to our innate negativity bias and the empty-seeming wardrobe.

Be honest: instead of telling yourself you're going shopping, say you're going out for a dopamine hit. Listen to your gut: if it's fluttering with butterflies and your heart is racing, it's the hormones doing the buying.

Check your feelings: are you shopping for comfort, for emotional distraction, because it's easier to change your look than to deal with what you feel?

Get angry: remind yourself about the real price of new things – think of the dolphins and the planet and the patriarchy and your wasted time…

Translate it: make a habit of translating from sales speak into plain English. For example, "sale" means "we need to shift this now because the stuff we want to sell you next is about to arrive". "Save on luxury cashmere" means "it's spring time".

Zoom out: think about how fashion looks from the moon, how when you shop you are like a little squirrel scurrying around collecting nuts. Or think about something that happens really slowly, like lichen growing in the tundra or trees turning into rock, to put your purchase into perspective.

Game it: set some rules that turn shopping into an ingenuity test. For example, you can only buy second hand, in charity shops or with at least 50% off. Don't buy things full price – it only encourages the sellers.

Get it on: if some garment is eating a hole in you, try it on your body – often that knocks the idea on the head and pricks the balloon of the transformational myth, the fantasy that you'll feel both complete and completely different if you buy it.

Cool off: walk away and think about it for a day or two, even if the shop won't hold the dress for you or they say it's the last one in that size. Give the hormones a chance to calm down and look in your wardrobe to remind yourself what you already have. And check the Pending Shelf, too.

Relocate it: if you saw the same item in a charity shop, would you still want it? Would you still want it without the label in it? These questions help you separate the clothes from the selling environment – beautiful shop, solicitous assistants, nice website etc.

Time-travel: in five years' time, will you be glad you own this thing? Can you even be sure you will next year? Do you want someone else to have to deal with it when you're dead? (A bit drastic, I know, but at my age it works.)

Look in the mirror: no, not at the clothes you're trying on. At your face. Do you look anxious or happy? That should tell you all you need to know about whether this potential purchase is about your own pleasure or the quest for social approval.

Look east: the Japanese have a word, *kuchisabishii*, which means eating because the mouth is lonely, as opposed to out of genuine hunger. Are you doing the sartorial equivalent, consuming to fill a void?

Change the voice: recast your inner critic as a character you don't like, preferably one you're already angry with. If, for example, Donald Trump doesn't think you look great, that's a positive! And who cares if Vladimir Putin doesn't like those old trousers on you?

Reframe it: see fashion as a bad relationship, a lover who makes you feel good at first, but turns out to be manipulative, bullying and controlling. Try seeing the entire fashion industry as a pimp who wants you not for yourself but only for the money you make him. That might make it less appealing to fall into its embrace.

Don't be told: Clothes = what we wear. Style = what we choose to wear. Fashion = what we're told to wear.

A new wardrobe

Let's time-travel together and stand in front of the ideal wardrobe of the future. I will guess what we might see in it.

- Fewer clothes, many of them second hand.

- Comfortable clothes that don't hurt or constrain us, truss us up or trip us up.

- Clothes that are pleasing but not man-pleasing.

- Clothes that have been made without exploiting workers in faraway lands or harming the planet.

- Clothes bought because they are loved, not because the fashion industry needs to flog them. (You remember fast fashion – it used to be in all those vacant shops on the high street?)

- Clothes without designer labels, because nobody cares about them any more (and none of those scratchy labels inside either).

- Clothes that have been chosen to celebrate the body, not to hide bits of it – clothes that cover the wearer not in shame but in glory.

Hard to imagine, isn't it? And yet there are signs that the cultural tide is turning. In 2017, France made it illegal to use excessively skinny models: the health ministry's aim was to fight eating disorders and inaccessible ideals of beauty. Around us today we see plus-size models and models of diverse skin colour and ethnicity – not enough maybe, but better than none (in 2018, a model wearing a hijab appeared for the first time on the cover of British *Vogue*). We see gender-non-conforming bodies and unisex clothing for sale. We see adverts using "real people" (aren't all people real?) and so-called quirky models, with ears that stick out or strong noses or wide-set eyes, who remind us of the variety of human appearance. We see campaigns calling for companies to tell us when images have been retouched and no-filter movements online. We see small companies focused on sustainable fashion and mass-market brands selling clothes labelled as fairtrade, slavery-free, ethically sourced. We see the pre-loved and rental market booming, and even clothing that doesn't exist, like the emperor's new clothes: branded fashions that can be purchased (with real money) in virtual worlds to be worn by avatars – the last gasp of designer madness, perhaps?

All of which looks like a promising start for the wardrobe of the future, but may, of course, just be dancing around on the tip of the iceberg that is destined to crush us. Only time will tell. And despite any recent changes, the basic premise of the garment industry remains the same: to sell stuff.

Curbing the urge to consume? To shop away our fears? I'm afraid that's still on us.

Something to wear

My teenage instinct that there was something bad about loving clothes was right, but I misdiagnosed the causes. Most of them, it turns out, are outside me rather than inside, or else so deeply embedded in my brain as to be nothing to do with me personally.

I hope I've shown that your wardrobe – whether it's the flat-pack or the walk-in variety – is far more than just a place for storing your clothes. Rather, it is a conflict zone where epic struggles are taking place and our atavistic fears are routinely triggered, and where our bodies have been commercialised more than Christmas. Above all, it is a piece of furniture that, like the heel tip of a stiletto, concentrates in one spot the heavy weight of the expectations, past and present, placed upon women.

Thank you for accompanying me on this journey through the wardrobe. I hope I haven't taken the fun out of clothes: I didn't set out to be a killjoy (and perhaps, anyway, they will be more fun now we understand them better). But I reasoned there are plenty of places where you can find instructions on how and where to get this season's look – and perhaps not so many trying to uncover the darker side of getting dressed. And I want to reiterate that I am not judging. None of what I've written here means that I don't find myself browsing the internet or wandering to the shops when I feel bored or dissatisfied or stressed or sad. I look in the fridge for the same reasons.

I set out to gain a better understanding of why we feel we have nothing to wear and why new things don't fix our feelings or give us a lasting sense of our own worth. And I hope that, like me, you now feel that you can stand up to the dictates of fashion just as vigorously as you would to any other form of dictatorship.

I'm not suggesting that we shouldn't love clothes, just that the medicine (shopping) needs to be appropriate to the ailment (feeling we have nothing to wear). And it is simply not possible to resolve the conflicts being played out in the wardrobe by acquiring more stuff, whether we do it online or in the high street, alone or with a personal shopper, on Bond Street or in the supermarket. The solution to wardrobe dysmorphia, like body dysmorphia, lies in our heads and not in the shops. The clothes we already own remain the exactly the same: what changes is our minds.

If there was a pill that could cure you of loving clothes, would you take it? I don't think I would. Whatever the puritans and moralists have said down the ages, and still do today, there is nothing inherently wrong with being interested in how you look: it is a profound part of being human. So we can ditch all that guilt. There is nothing wrong with making the most of ourselves, with one very important condition: that we ensure, as far as humanly possible, that we ourselves get to decide precisely what "making the most of ourselves" looks like.

We can't make that decision without awareness, and I hope this book has given you some of that, and even perhaps some immunity to the more harmful effects of the fashion virus. I hope it has made you fashion conscious, not in the old sense of knowing what's in fashion, but in a new one that means being fully aware of how fashion works and what it does to us.

Lastly, let's resolve to appreciate our bodies not for the way they look, but for the way they look after us (breathing, pumping blood around, that kind of thing). Because clothes look best on a body that is loved.

Pause. Breathe.

Maybe don't click and buy. Perhaps the card stays in the wallet.

Open the wardrobe.

See that it is full.

Bibliography

In reverse alphabetical order (if you don't know why, ask someone whose surname begins with W):

Wilson, Elizabeth, and Taylor, Lou. *Through the Looking Glass: A History of Dress from 1860 to the Present Day* (BBC Books, London, 1989)

Williams, Mark, and Penman, Danny. *Deeper Mindfulness* (Piatkus, London, 2023)

Tilberis, Liz. *No Time To Die* (Weidenfeld & Nicolson, London, 1998)

Siegel, Ronald D, *The Mindfulness Solution* (The Guilford Press, New York, 2010)

Siegle, Lucy. *To Die For: Is Fashion Wearing Out the World* (Fourth Estate, London, 2011)

Ribeiro, Aileen, with Blackman, Cally. *Six Centuries of Dress at the National Portrait Gallery* (NPG Publications, London, 2015)

Orbach, Susie. *Bodies* (Profile Books, London, 2009)

Monaghan, John, and Just, Peter. *Social & Cultural Anthropology* (Oxford University Press, Oxford, 2000)

Lurie, Alison, *The Language of Clothes* (Random House, New York, 1981)

Laver, James. *A Concise History of Costume* (Thames and Hudson, London, 1969) revised and retitled *Costume and Fashion: A Concise History* (1995, 2002 and 2012)

Harari, Yuval Noah. Sapiens: *A Brief History of Humankind* (Harvill Secker, London, 2014 - first publication in English)

French, Marilyn. *From Eve to Dawn: A History of Women, Volume 1: Origins* (McArthur & Company, Toronto, 2002)

Fraser, Antonia. *The Six Wives of Henry VIII* (Weidenfeld & Nicolson, London, 1992)

Feldman, Christina, and Kuyken, Willem. *Mindfulness: Ancient Wisdom meets Modern Psychology* (Guilford Press, New York, 2019)

Feldman Barrett, Lisa. *Seven and a Half Lessons about the Brain* (Houghton Mifflin Harcourt, New York, 2020)

Fashion: *The Ultimate Book of Costume and Style* (Dorling Kindersley, London, 2012)

Criado Perez, Caroline. *Invisible Women: Exposing Data Bias in a World Designed for Men* (Chatto & Windus, 2019)

Bryson, Bill. *At Home: A Short History of Private Life* (Doubleday, London, 2010)

Blakemore, Sarah-Jayne. *Inventing Ourselves: The Secret Life of the Teenage Brain* (Doubleday, London, 2018)

Berger, John. *Ways of Seeing* (BBC and Penguin Books, London, 1972)

The digital resources of the British Library, the V&A Museum, the Bodleian Library and the Smithsonian.

Acknowledgements

Without Tim de Lisle and Isabel Lloyd this book would not exist. At *Intelligent Life* magazine they let me write a column called "Applied Fashion" about clothing and its role in our lives, and I am indebted to them for their trust, example and editorial skill. Some of these chapters began life in that column and I am grateful to *The Economist* for permission to use this material, as well as to my former colleagues there, especially John Micklethwait, Ed Carr, Julie Kavanagh, Maggie Ferguson and Robert Butler.

This book would also not exist without the team at New River books. My sincerest thanks to Rebecca Nicolson for her advice and encouragement, to Catherine Gibbs for making things happen, and to Aurea Carpenter, a truly collaborative editor who can see not just the wood and the trees, but the forest and the splinter too. Deep thanks also to Katherine Stroud, Sam Suthurst and Helena Sutcliffe for bringing it into the light.

Thank you to Alexandra Shulman for saying I should write a book and to others I learned from in my many seasons at *Vogue*, notably Sarah Mower, Frances Bentley, Lisa Armstrong and Andrew Powell. I am also grateful to Professor Willem Kuyken for casting his learned eye over some of these chapters and to the Oxford Mindfulness Foundation; to my art teachers, especially Thomas Yeomans, Estelle Lovatt and Patricia Barker, for teaching me to look; to Nitza Spiro for her inspiring class about women in the Old Testament; to Dominique Cussem for her insights and her shop; and to Holly Ovenden for her strong and striking cover design.

Jean Gordon, Griz Gordon and Sarah Post read early drafts and made helpful comments. Many thanks to them and to the rest of my brilliant friends and relations (some of whom will recognise themselves in these pages) for being there and for many years of clothes talk: Pip Allen, Fay Ballard, Amelia Bullmore, Angie Butler, Liza Cawthorn, Graham Clempson, Anna Cryer, Flora de Falbe, Amanda de Lisle, Eliane Fattal, P Fiennes, Sarah Foot, Emma Forbes, Lucia Graham, Martha-Louise Hagerty, Sarah Halford, Christine Hanway, Miranda Harvey, Joey Jackson, Nicola King, Annabel Lea, Jessie Lea, Piers Lea, Clare Martin, Robin McCallum, Neil Midgley, Amelia Mendoza, Deepa Mer, Marion Milne, Katie Newton, Jo O'Driscoll, Matilda Pecover, William Pecover, Gillian Patterson, Elizabeth Peltz, Claire Shutes, Helen Simpson, Carol Skinner, Lucy Smouha, Jane Stewart, Kerri Summers, Karen Taylor, Eliza Thompson, Arabella Warburton, Elizabeth West, Araminta Whitley, Alex Willis, Catalina Willis, Marie-Christine Willis and Rio Vera.

My great gratitude goes to all of my amazing family: to my mother Claire, my siblings Simon, Fenella and Michela, to all my nephews and nieces and to my in-laws John and Jill.

And, last in this list but first in my heart, to Nick, Joe and Sam: my infinite appreciation and love.

Index